The Jews of Kaifeng, China:
history, culture, and religion

THE JEWS OF KAIFENG, CHINA:
HISTORY, CULTURE, AND RELIGION

By
Xu Xin

Ktav Publishing House, Inc.

Library of Congress Cataloging-in-Publication Data

Xu, Xin, 1949-
 The Jews of Kaifeng, China : history, culture, and religion / by Xu
Xin.
    p. cm.
Includes bibliographical references and index.
 ISBN 0-88125-791-5
 1. Jews--China--Kaifeng Shi--History. 2. Jews--China--Kaifeng
Shi--Social life and customs. 3. Jews--China--Kaifeng Shi--Identity.
4. Kaifeng Shi (China)--Ethnic relations. I. Title.
 DS135.C5X92 2003
 951'.18--dc21
                                      2002155395

                         Manufactured in the United States of America

                                Published by
                            KTAV Publishing House
                             930 Newark Avenue
                            Jersey City, NJ 07306
                            Email: info@ktav.com

To
Kong Defang

Contents

Preface

This book discusses the Chinese Jews of Kaifeng: their arrival, growth, success, way of life, faith, final decline, and the heritage they left behind. It traces the growth of a community that numbered no more than a few thousand at its height, recording their struggle for existence within and, at times, against the framework of the sociopolitical environment of the host country.

Why do we need another book on a subject already covered by numerous books and articles? Much that has been written about the Jews of China is fantasy; much is polemic, and much is, at best, pseudo-history. Little if any attention has been paid to charting the life of the Kaifeng Jewish community from a historical standpoint. This study undertakes to fill the gap.

As indicated by its title, this book is concerned primarily with social and religious history. Nonetheless, it also includes a consideration of the internal communal organization and life of the Kaifeng Jews and their relations with native Chinese.

Chapter 1 explains the social background for the formation of the Kaifeng Jewish community, laying the foundation for answers to such questions as "why China?" and "why Kaifeng?"

Chapter 2 depicts the history and life of Kaifeng Jewry against the general development of Chinese society. While this is of interest first and foremost to the student of Jewish history, it has meaning for the Chinese historian as well, since it reflects certain aspects of Chinese society and life from an unusual perspective.

Chapter 3 accounts for the inner life of Kaifeng Jewry. Almost no stone of the community's inner life is untouched. The description demonstrates that the Kaifeng Jewish community was not much different from any other Jewish community in the world as far as its inner life was concerned.

Chapter 4 examines the identity of Kaifeng Jewry. The analysis of the attitudes, beliefs, and ritual practices that conditioned the identity of the Kaifeng Jews shows to what extent they were able to retain their faith intact.

Chapter 5 treats the relations of the Kaifeng Jews with their Chinese neighbors and with the government. It also discusses the local Muslim community and contacts with Christians of various denominations.

Chapter 6 provides a brief account of the Jewish communities in other Chinese cities.

The sources for a study of this kind vary widely. There is little documentary evidence for the early period. There are only occasional references to Jews in Chinese sources. Jewish sources, while not copious, are useful, but most of the available sources were not written or created by the Kaifeng Jews themselves. Legends, inscriptions, histories, biographies, religious texts, and travelers' stories all contribute to our knowledge about the Kaifeng Jews.

One of the tasks of the historian is to ferret out these bits of information, evaluate them, and fit them into their places in the puzzle. The methods for this type of historical reconstruction are complex and often hotly debated, involving opposing theories and philosophies of history. This mixture of fact and legend is a striking example of how a naive group fashions actual happenings into something strange and romantic. But, shorn of all possible fanciful elements, the story is romantic enough and perhaps unique in the history of the Jewish people. However, synthetic comprehensive historical works are usually based on available materials and studies rather than on original research in primary sources. Whatever studies had been done before the start of this work serve as its foundation and base. In working on this book, I utilized the accessible sources, compared them, and made my own choices based on prior research and study.

A Chinese proverb says, "Make the past serve the present," Kaifeng remains one of the most colorful threads once worked into the rich pattern of the Chinese tapestry. Perhaps this and other scholarship may inspire a small but active community of Jews to return to Kaifeng to keep alive China's reputation for hospitality and friendship. Kindness to strangers has been for long centuries the characteristic of China, as indeed it is one of the supreme duties enjoined on Jews by their religious beliefs.

Xu Xin
December 17, 2002
Nanjing University, Nanjing, China

Acknowledgments

I am most grateful to Dr. Alfred Gottschalk, former president of Hebrew Union College, and Professor Ruth Wiesse, former director of the Center for Jewish Studies at Harvard University, for inviting me to do research at their institutions and providing me with financial aid for my research and writing this book in 1995 and 1996. The visiting scholar status I had at both Hebrew Union College and Harvard made it possible for me to use the rich resources and facilities at those institutions, which were essential for the completion of this study.

I wish to express my sincerest thanks to Dr. Beverly Friend, an emeritus professor of Oakton Community College, for her wise advice and great efforts to polish my English writings as always. Her intelligence and sense of style have contributed much to the manuscript. Without her scholarly linguistic assistance, the book would never look like what it is now.

I am indebted to all the authors whose works I either used as references or quoted in writing the book. I am particularly grateful to Donald D. Leslie and Michael Pollak, two outstanding scholars in the study of Kaifeng Jewry. Their works inspired me to start this project. I am extremely indebted to them for their generous permissions to quote freely from their writings.

I would like to acknowledge the following publishers and authors who were kind enough to give permission to quote from their publications:

E.J. Brill: *The Survival of the Chinese Jews*, 1975

Jewish Publication Society: *Mandarins, Jews, and Missionaries*, 1980

Hippocrene Books: *Jews in Old China*, 1984

University of Toronto Press: *Chinese Jews*, 1942

Ariel Publications: *Ariel*, 1991, No. 84

I am very grateful to Mr. Bernard Scharfstein, editor-in-chief of KTAV Publishing House, who not only published my first book in English, *Legends of the Chinese Jews of Kaifeng*, but also encouraged me to write this book. This book would not have been written without his encouragement.

I wish also to thank Mr. and Mrs. Richard Scheuer and The Simon and Helen Scheuer Family Foundation for providing additional funds for my research at Harvard in 1996. Their support made my life easier and more comfortable to concentrate on my study.

My gratitude should also go to Nanjing University for providing released time that enabled me to complete this book in the United States.

Lastly, more than anyone else, I wish to thank my wife, Kong Defang, whose patience during the writing of this book was often tested, for her understanding and support of my scholarly studies.

Chapter One

China and Chinese Society
When the Jews Arrived

DISCOVERY

If not for a chance meeting between a Chinese Jew and a Jesuit priest in the year 1605, the Western world might never have known about the isolated Jewish community that flourished in China for many centuries.

The story of the meeting, which sounds incredible but is fully documented, tells the tale of an encounter between Ai Tien, a Jew from the city of Kaifeng in northern China, and an Italian Jesuit named Matteo Ricci.

While in Peking hoping for assignment to the imperial civil service after having successfully completed the magistrate's examination, Ai learned of a book entitled *Things I Have Heard Told* about a small band of Europeans headed by Ricci who were starting a church. The book said that the foreigners believed in one god.

Most educated Chinese would have assumed that the foreigners were Muslims, the only monotheists known to them, but Ai, who was a Jew, thought that they too might be Jews. He went to the Jesuit church thinking it a synagogue and introduced himself to Ricci, whom he took to be a rabbi. Ricci, who had been searching for Christian communities in China, assumed that Ai was a Christian and greeted him with open arms.

Because the celebration of the festival of St. John the Baptist was underway, a painting of a youthful St. John together with Mary and the infant Jesus had been placed near the altar. Ricci knelt before them. Ai knew nothing of Christianity but was familiar with the stories of the biblical patriarchs. Assuming that the figures in the painting were Rebekah and her sons Jacob and Esau, he too knelt, although kneeling to pray was not his usual custom. Later, seeing a mural of Matthew, Mark, Luke, and John, he wondered aloud if they might not be four of the twelve sons of Jacob and asked where the other eight were.

Confusion piled upon confusion, but finally everything was sorted out, leaving Ricci disappointed at not having found a Chinese Christian, but astounded to have found a Chinese Jew.

Ricci had discovered a Diaspora with an amazing history possibly dating from the eleventh-century migrations of Jewish merchants and traders along the Silk Road from Persia and India. The religious life of the Jews of Kaifeng, he learned, was centered on the synagogue. The Jewish community in Kaifeng included families that observed most of the traditional festivals, abstained from eating pork, circumcised their sons, and followed the laws of Moses in ways similar to the practices of Jews in Europe. Because of the community's isolation, however, it faced the threat of assimilation.

When Ricci sent messengers to Kaifeng with Ai, they carried a letter for the chief rabbi telling him that the Jesuit house of worship in Peking had all the books of the Hebrew Bible, and, as well, a set of later scriptures called the New Testament. This, he explained, would be of special interest to the Kaifeng Jews because in it they would finally be able to read the story of the Messiah who had come sixteen centuries earlier to redeem them and all of the world's other peoples.

On reading this, the bemused rabbi responded that he did not understand how a man of Ricci's vast erudition could believe that the Messiah had already arrived when it was common knowledge that he had not and would not for another ten thousand years. The rabbi added, however, that he himself was now old and frail, and would be willing to let Ricci succeed him as chief rabbi if he moved to Kaifeng.

The rabbi was less concerned with Ricci's seemingly aberrant belief in the Messiah (which he took to be a personal idiosyncrasy) than with his disobedience to the dietary laws and said that the job was his if he would give up eating pork.

Ricci, of course, knew a great deal about Jews and Judaism, both from his education in Bible and Christian history, and from having encountered real Jews in Europe and elsewhere, but the Jews of Kaifeng had never heard of Christianity. Ai Tien seems to have concluded that Christianity was a Jewish sect that had certain peculiar doctrines and practices but was still a part of the House of Israel.

Ricci, for his part, thought that the Kaifeng Jewish community was on the verge of extinction, but he was wrong. Seven or eight more generations of Jews were still to live out their lives in the former capital of the Song emperors before the community ceased to function as a viable religious entity. And even after that, among their descendants, there was nostalgic evocation of the traditions and ethnic origins of their forebears leading to at least a nominal allegiance to the ancient faith.

This book is devoted to exploring the tale of Kaifeng Jewry: how Jews came to China and settled in Kaifeng, and what we know—or can surmise—of their history.

BACKGROUND

Before answering the questions "Why China?" and "Why Kaifeng?" as we begin to trace Jewish life in this distant part of the world, it is necessary, first, to place China in geographical and historical focus, with the main emphasis on the period of the Tang and Song dynasties, the era when Jews began to settle in China.

Chinese Civilization and Xi'an

As the biggest and most important empire of the Orient, China has an uninterrupted history going back nearly five thousand years. Its tremendous cultural influence is not due simply to the size of its population or the extent of its territory, but to the remarkable continuity of Chinese civilization. In contrast, the Western cultural stream chronicles the rise and fall of successive nations that each in turn made contributions and then receded into comparative obscurity.

Equally important, just as the Jewish cultural tradition has been of world-historical significance in certain spheres, so too Chinese civilization has had a strong impact on the development of world civilization. For centuries, the Chinese viewed themselves as more culturally advanced than their neighbors, an island of civilization in the midst of a sea of "barbarians," and so they coined the term "Middle Kingdom" for their homeland.

As early as the fourth to third centuries B.C.E. trade seems to have developed between China and Mongolia and Central Asia. This trade increased during the Han dynasty (206 B.C.E.–ca. 220 C.E.). The trade in silk across the Eurasian continent grew even greater in the first and second centuries. The lands involved included countries in the western regions: Central Asia, northern India, the Parthian Empire, and the Roman Empire. The famous Silk Road linked the valley of the Yellow River to the Mediterranean and points even farther west.

During the Tang dynasty (618–907), while Europe was going through its Dark Ages, China reached one of the peaks in its history, both culturally and economically. Xi'an (then called Chang'an), the royal seat of the dynasty, was "the veritable cultural capital of East Asia and the largest city by far in the world. So powerful was its influence that it served as the model for the capitals of other contemporary East Asian states, notably Parbae and Japan."[1]

Moreover, China was not only a culturally prosperous, scientifically advanced country, but an open society. Since the Han dynasty, it had sent envoys to many countries and welcomed foreign visitors, whether traders or diplomats. Communication between China and the world was frequent and smooth. The expansion of the Tang dynasty in Central Asia, up to the borders of Iran, was not sudden and unforeseeable. To the contrary, it was preceded at the time of the first Turkish incursions into North China by a period of great diplomatic activity in the empire. This is proved by the number of embassies that appeared in Xi'an. "People from all over the world congregated there, including diplomatic envoys, religious missionaries, merchants, and students. With them came foreign religions such as Zoroastrianism, Manichaeanism, and Nestorian Christianity and associated places of worship."[2]

Due to the presence of so many traders, diplomats, missionaries, and scholars from other countries during the Tang period, from the eighth to the tenth century, the Chinese became accustomed to the sight of foreigners, many of whom had settled in the cities of Northwest China. Their presence there is verified by ample evidence of the importation of statues, gems, and ornaments of Mediterranean origin. The Chinese government tolerated the establishment of foreign religions, with the result that Xi'an, the country's capital, was the site of houses of worship devoted to Nestorian Christianity, Manichaeism, Islam, and Zoroastrianism. Meanwhile, foreign trading communities were also growing in Canton, Quanzhou, Yangzhou, and other cities in South or East China.

Attracted by China's rich culture, quite a few of the visitors and merchants who came for business or pleasure decided to settle there permanently. The large number of Muslim communities built up in Chinese cities during the Tang dynasty provides strong evidence of this immigration. China was a great melting pot, attracting settlers from many other lands. Indeed, throughout history,

China's ability to absorb people from other cultures has been amazing. Foreign conquerors ended up conquered by the Chinese way of life, adopting China's culture and language rather than trying to impose their own cultural identity.

From the official Chinese viewpoint, all foreign settlers were designated "Chinese minorities" even though they belonged to different nationalities. When the Manchu people, who originated in northeastern China, defeated the Han Chinese, the country's ethnic majority, and founded the Qing dynasty (1644–1911), they were assimilated. Like the Romans, who defeated the Greeks in battle and in politics but learned from them culturally, the Manchus studied Chinese culture, learned the Chinese language, and adopted the Chinese way of life. Today, the descendants of the Manchus have forgotten their ancestral tongue and speak only Chinese.

The influx of foreign settlers enriched China considerably. It is no exaggeration to say that during the Tang dynasty, the 287 years the Tang emperors occupied the throne, China was probably the most civilized country on earth. Thus one of the brightest eras of the East coincided with the darkest days of the West, when Europe was wrapped in the ignorance and degradation of the Middle Ages. There are several explanations for this. One holds that while geographically China is at the easternmost end of the world, her connections with the many nations to the west were always open. The major channel of communication and commerce was the Silk Road, a system of transcontinental trade routes connecting eastern and western Eurasia via central Eurasia. Prior to the opening of sea routes toward the end of the Middle Ages, the Silk Road linked China with Central and Western Asia as far as the eastern shores of the Mediterranean. The route was opened for traffic in the second century B.C.E. and remained in use until the late thirteenth century, when it was abandoned because advances in ship design and navigation made sea routes safer and more convenient.

The Silk Road began in the Chinese city of Xi'an, extended westward through the long and narrow Hexi Strip, forked into two routes along the northern and southern edges of the Tallimakan Desert, crossed the Pamir, and passed through Central and Western Asia to the eastern coast of the Mediterranean. People from the West think of the Silk Road as having ended up in Xi'an, but in Chinese eyes Xi'an was the road's starting point. It's all a matter of perspective.

In his *Illustration of the Western World*, written during the Sui dynasty at the beginning of the seventh century, Pei Ju, a Chinese historian, describes the Silk Road in great detail. There were three main routes from Tunhuang to the Mediterranean.[3] The northernmost went through the region inhabited by the Khazars, a Turkic people that converted to Judaism and Islam in the eighth century, to Byzantium (Constantinople); the middle route stretched across Persia; the southern one crossed northern India, connected with the middle one at Baghdad, then went on to the ports of Tyre and Acre on the Mediterranean coast.

In the thirteenth century, two Venetian merchants, Niccolo and Matteo Polo, made their way to China via the northern route. They set out from Constantinople, crossed Khazaria into Central Asia, then went south via Bukhara and Samarkand, and arrived in Hami. On their second journey, accompanied by Niccolo's son Marco Polo, who later wrote an account of his experiences in China, they departed from the port of Acre (Akko) in Palestine, followed the southern route by way of Balh and Khotan, and arrived in the capital of the Yuan dynasty.[4]

As a thoroughfare of commerce and trade, the Silk Road played an important role in connecting East and West. The route was pioneered in 139 B.C.E. by an adventurous Chinese official named Zhang Qian, who journeyed to the western regions. Legend tells, as well, of a western merchant, an emissary from the Roman emperor Marcus Aurelius (121–180 C.E.), who traveled the full length of

the Silk Road to offer elephant tusks, rhinoceros horns, and tor-
toise shell to the Chinese, testifying to the growing economic and
cultural exchange between East and West.

.To the peoples of the West, especially the Romans, the main
attraction of China was silk, which is how this famous trade route
got its name. Silk became fashionable in Rome as early as the first
century B.C.E.

A third-century C.E. Roman historian, Solinus, wrote: "It was
the passion for luxury that led first women and now even men to
use these fabrics which serve to reveal the body rather than to
clothe it."[5] When Julius Caesar (100–44 B.C.E.) once appeared in
the theater dressed in a splendid toga of Chinese silk, his garment
attracted everybody's attention. The demand for this fabric promoted much profitable trade along the Silk Road, which continued
even after the fall of the Roman Empire.

The lucrative profits from the silk trade brought exceptional
prosperity to the cities of medieval Central Asia. Persians and
Arabs dominated the trade, but Jews was quite active in it as well,
for there were many Jewish settlements in the area. The Jews of the
region were mainly weavers and dyers of cotton cloth and silk.
Jewish merchants known as Radhanites regularly engaged in trade
on the Silk Road and often guided its caravans.[6]

As the Israeli historian Menashe Har-El notes:

According to the Babylonian Talmud, the Jews settled in
cities along the Silk Road in the fourth century C.E. at the
latest. The common Aramaic language encouraged the settlement of the Jews and their involvement in the international trade of silk and silk dyeing. The Tang dynasty in
China was receptive to foreign religions and invited the Jews
to settle in the country. A Chinese document of the ninth
century C.E. notes that the Jewish merchants spoke many

languages: Arabic, Persian, Latin, French, Spanish and Slavic. During this period, the Chinese used bilingual coins with Chinese inscriptions on one side and Semitic letters on the other.[7]

The role of Jewish merchants and traders along the Silk Road is also described by Martin Gilbert:

Jewish merchants played a leading part in trade after the fall of the Roman Empire. A Persian writer in about 850 AD recorded the journeys of the Jewish traders known as "Radanites" who linked the Frankish and Chinese kingdoms by land and sea. Their name probably comes from a Persian phrase meaning "knowing the way."[8]

Donald D. Leslie adds:

We have clear evidence of Jewish communities at many of the overland posting stations as far as Khorassan, "the Gateway to China." That Jews joined those going further is suggested by the Judeo-Persian fragment found in Dandan Uiliq, and by the page of Hebrew prayers found in Tun-huang, both of about the 9th Century. It is worth pointing out . . . that at a time of Christian-Moslem animosity, when many trade-routes were blocked, Jews were the best equipped to carry out the trade from Asia to Europe.[9]

Besides the Silk Road, which connected China and the coun-tries to its west by land, the sea routes from the Persian Gulf, across the Indian Ocean, to the various provinces of southeastern China were soon opened and used by merchants. Once again, most of them were Persians and Arabs, but there was also a sizable Jewish contingent.

The tenth century was a transitional time of turmoil in Chinese history. The once-powerful and unified Tang dynasty fell apart because of civil strife. The country broke up into five states. War and battle was the order of the day. This situation did not last long, however. After about half a century of disorder, the country was reunited, but under a different banner—that of the Song dynasty, which came to power officially in the year 960.

The new dynasty worked very hard to promote a more stable society. As a result, Chinese culture developed rapidly. An agricultural and commercial revolution based on technological developments brought greatly increased productivity. Many measures were introduced to emphasize trade and promote business. The revival of trade and of urban centers, cities and towns, vitally affected the living standards of China's people and opened relations between China and other countries.

The emperors of the Song dynasty maintained the same open-door policy toward foreigners as had the Tang emperors. As a result, Arabs, Persians, and other peoples came to China by the thousands, and many of them settled in cities across the country.

Technological advances brought about important changes in the conduct of foreign trade. Among the innovations introduced in the Song period were the application of the compass to marine navigation and the wider use of the stern-post rudder. Chinese shipbuilders were now able to construct junks that could sail the high seas more safely and more efficiently. Chinese vessels were now able to carry exports as far as the coast of Africa. At the same time, communities of foreigners were being established in cities on China's southern coast. Quanzhou (the city Marco Polo called Zaitun) and Fuzhou succeeded Canton as major trade centers. All this put China in a position to be open to the rest of the world.

The most important and prosperous city of the Song dynasty was its capital, Kaifeng, which was then was called Bianliang.

KAIFENG

The historic city of Kaifeng is situated in what is now Henan Province, a few miles south of the Yellow River, the second-largest river in China as well as in Asia. Since 560, the year it was opened, the Grand Canal has provided the city with easy communications and transportation, thus increasing its importance as a commercial center.

Kaifeng served as the capital of the state of Wei in the third century. During the Five Dynasties period (907–960) it was the capital of Zhuo, one of the powerful dynasties. However, it was during the Northern Song dynasty (960–1126) that it attained its greatest fame and became an opulent and prosperous metropolis, attracting Jewish merchants and traders.

In order to better understand why Zhao Kuangyin, the first emperor of the Song dynasty, chose Kaifeng as his capital and made it the center of his realm, let us quote the description of the city penned by a poet of the Song period, Qin Guan (1049–1100), who actually lived there:

> Kaifeng, surrounded by level land in all directions, is a convergence of roads which connect it with the Chu River to the south, the Han River to the west, the Zhao River to the north, and the Qi River to the east. Neither great mountain ranges nor big rivers isolate it from the surrounding regions; in fact its communication with them is aided by the Bian and Cai and other rivers. These waterways teem with boats, the bow of one touching the stern of another, while men, carts and animals jam the roads in an endless flow from every corner of the country.[10]

After dredging, the Bian River was connected with the Yangtze and the Huai, thus permitting direct transportation of huge amounts of merchandise on vessels of every size from all points of the compass:

> ... the Bian River carries every year several million piculs of tribute rice, shipping from Hunan, Hubei and Zhenjiang provinces via the Yangtze and the Hui rivers. And the products transported in from the southeastern area and other places are incalculable.[11]

Zhou Bangyan (1057–1121), another renowned poet of the Song period, depicts a river spectacle in his "Ode to Kaifeng":

One thousand Li, stern crowding bow,
A hundred types of vessels flow,
   Sails a-bulge when winds are fair,
   In rain punt poles thrust everywhere.
Boatmen chanting, accents broad,
In twos and threes the craft sweep for'd,
   As trumpets shout,
   Drums pound,
   And bells ring out
   In clamorous sound.[12]

Compounding the advantages of its location, the emperor ordered the city rebuilt and enlarged to make it the jewel of his realm. Before long, it was not only the political center of the country, but its economic center—a flourishing metropolis with a population of more than a million and a rendezvous for traders and merchants. There were 6,400 shops in Kaifeng. The following description gives us a of sense of its prosperity:

> To the east was Panlou Street, on the southern side of which was "Eagles' Inn," which accommodated only traders in hawks and falcons. Here also were shops selling pearls, silk,

joss-sticks, medicinal herbs, and mats. The street turns south into Jie Shen Lane, where trade in gold, silver, and colored silks was transacted. The buildings, with broad open fronts, were awesome to the common people. A single deal could run into the astonishing sum of ten million strings of cash. These traders and merchants were doubtless multi-millionaires.[13]

The French scholar Jacques Gernet emphasizes Kaifeng's cosmopolitan character as a commercial city:

K'aifeng provides the first example of a popular agglomeration in which commercial life and amusements were predominant. The political organs and their staff found themselves from this time onwards in direct contact with a typically urban population consisting mainly of the lower classes, while the commercial upsurge broke all the old rules which tended to preserve the aristocratic character of the city. The curfew was abolished at K'aifeng in 1063 and from them onwards people could move about freely during the night. Businesses and places of entertainment remained open until dawn.[14]

The city's unplanned and unregulated growth during this period, when its population rose to more than a million, contrasted sharply with the orderly layout of China's previous capitals, but reflected the dramatic commercial development of the day.

As the main commercial center of China in this era, Kaifeng, like Xi'an during the Tang dynasty, attracted merchants and traders not only from all over the country, but from the whole world. Historical documents tell that the city was frequently visited by merchants and traders from Korea, Kampuchea, Japan, and the countries of Central Asia, Arabia, and Europe. It is recorded in the sources that envoys from Dashi (Arabia) visited China twenty-four times during the Song dynasty; many of them were actually merchants serving as emissaries. *Reminiscences*, a well-known book

about the history and life of Kaifeng, describes some of these out-
landers as they appeared at an imperial morning audience one New
Year's Day:

> The emissary from Great Liao wore a golden hat with a broad
> brim curling upwards like a lotus leaf, a fitted purple robe,
> and gold-thread-plaited boots. The deputy emissary was clad
> in Han style in a robe bound at the waist with a gold-thread-
> ed belt. Both the emissary and the deputy emissary of the Xia
> State wore golden hats, short and close-fitting scarlet robes
> and gold-thread-plaited boots. They bowed with crossed
> hands. . . . The Huibes (Uygurs) had long beards and high
> noses, and wore turbans and caps. The Khotans wore flower-
> patterned gold-threaded felt hats and gold-threaded robes
> with belts around their waists. They brought their wives and
> children with them, all riding camels with jingling bronze
> bells, to pay tribute to the Song Court.[15]

In short, in the era when Jews began migrating to its capital,
China was unlike the countries of medieval Europe. By and large,
Western society was underdeveloped and uncultivated, with a very
primitive, even barbaric, social structure. In contrast, China was a
sophisticated, highly centralized feudalistic power, militarily strong
and technologically advanced. Culturally, it was a polished, civilized society deeply rooted in Confucianism. A civil service system
several hundred years old, which selected government officials on
the basis of a series of imperial examinations, had become well
established.

It was such a place and situation that the Jews found when they
arrived in Kaifeng and eventually chose to settle there permanently.

[1] *Encyclopedia of Asian History*, vol. 1, p. 248.

[2] Ibid., p. 249.

[3] *Sui Annals*, vol. 67, biography of Pei Ju.

[4] Gong Fangzhen, "The Jewish Merchants on the Silk Road," p. 2.

[5] Solinus, *Polyhistor*, 51.

[6] Har-El, in *Ariel*, No. 84 (1991), pp. 8–9.

[7] Ibid., pp. 16–17.

[8] Gilbert, *Atlas of Jewish History*, p. 22.

[9] Leslie, *Survival of the Chinese Jews*, p. 5.

[10] Jiang Qingxiang and Xiao Guoliang, "Glimpses of the Urban Economy of Bianjing, Capital of the Northern Song Dynasty, as Seen in the Painting *Riverside Scene at Clear and Bright Festival Time* and the Book *Reminiscences of Dreamland Glories of the Eastern Capital*"; English version quoted from Shapiro, *Jews in Old China*, p. 104.

[11] Ibid., p. 105.

[12] Ibid., pp. 105–106.

[13] Ibid., p. 107.

[14] Gernet, *History of Chinese Civilization*, p. 317.

[15] Shapiro, *Jews in Old China*, p. 113.

Chapter Two

The History

THE BEGINNINGS

When did Jews first arrive in Kaifeng? No definitive answer can be given. All that can be said is that Jews came to China from several places at various times in the medieval period or earlier. However, while China's other foreign communities grew up gradually over time, the Jewish settlement in Kaifeng apparently was established all at once by a core group that obtained official permission to live there permanently, construct a synagogue, and establish a normative Jewish life in the city. Thus, although individual Jews may have come to Kaifeng separately from time to time, the history of Kaifeng's Jewry is essentially the continuous story of a single homogeneous community over a period of several centuries.

The question of Jewish origins in Kaifeng, a controversial subject to this day, was first raised in the early seventeenth century by Matteo Ricci, the Jesuit priest who learned of the existence of Kaifeng Jewry in 1605 and sent the news to Europe. While documentation about the community's early years is sparse, there are at least some materials, however incomplete and tantalizing, unlike the case for some other equally isolated Jewish communities, such as the Bene Israel, the Cochin Jews, and the Jews of Ethiopia. Some of the material is legendary, some of a more historical nature. Taken together it enables historians to partially reconstruct and describe the beginnings of Kaifeng's Jewish community.

LEGENDARY SOURCES

Legends are often the most interesting quasi-historical records. The traditions of the Kaifeng Jews regarding their arrival in the city can be sensational and romantic. One oral tradition tells of a caravan of several hundred Jewish merchants and craftsmen with their families and their possessions, reaching the capital of the Song emperors after a long journey that began somewhere on the Mediterranean coast.[1] Another popular legend indicates that it was in obedience to a divine command that the Jews came to Kaifeng.[2]

These tales, though lacking a factual basis and undoubtedly invented in much later times, contain a grain of historical truth in that they indicate the existence of a Jewish community in the city and point to its origin.

A considerable body of conjectures and hypotheses exists about the origin of the Kaifeng Jews. Suggested dates for the beginnings of Kaifeng Jewry range from biblical times to the twelfth century C.E.

As mentioned in Chapter 1, the Jewish movement to China started quite early, perhaps during the Han dynasty (206 B.C.E.–ca. 220 C.E) or earlier, as some scholars believe, and continued throughout the Middles Ages. One theory holds that Jewish settlers arrived from Persia during the reign of Emperor Ming Di of the Han dynasty (sometime between 58 and 75 C.E.).

N. M. Adler, in his *Chinese Jews*, adduced the existence of a Jewish colony around 34 C.E.[3]

The great historian Heinrich Graetz maintained that large numbers of Jews arrived in 231 C.E. as a result of persecution in Persia.[4]

This date is confirmed by Father Gaubil, a French Jesuit who visited Kaifeng in the eighteenth century, and reported that the city's Jews told him their ancestors had entered China 1,650 years earlier from Xi-yu (Persia).[5]

Kong Xianyi, a Chinese historian from Kaifeng, asserts that Jews first settled there during the Tang dynasty, when the city became an important regional commercial center. He points out that they continued to live in the city after it became the Song capital even though a Song law required that foreign communities had to be located outside the city. This seems to indicate that the Jews were residents before the Song dynasty.[6] Although plausible, there is no evidence to back this assertion.

The Kaifeng Jews themselves gave an account of their arrival in an inscription they erected in 1489, although some scholars point out that they gave conflicting information in other surviving sources. For instance, while the 1489 inscription that states that they arrived during the Song dynasty (960–1279), another inscription, dating from 1512, says that they arrived during the Han dynasty (206 B.C.E.–ca. 220 C.E.), and the 1663 inscription states that it was during the Zhou period (ca. 1066 B.C.E.–256 B.C.E.).[7] However, analysis of the statements in the 1512 and 1663 inscriptions shows that these citations actually deal with the year of entry of Judaism into China, not with the time of the arrival of Jews in the city.

In any case, scholars and historians agree almost unanimously that it was during the Song dynasty (960–1279) that the Jews came to Kaifeng and founded a community there. The question now is whether it is possible to find out more precisely when they arrived, since the Song dynasty lasted more than three hundred years. Presumably it was before 1126, because it was only during the Northern Song period, from 960 to 1126, that Kaifeng was the dynasty's capital. The Song court abandoned the city after its defeat by the Tartars and moved south in 1127.

It is hard to imagine that newly arriving Jews would have chosen to live in Kaifeng after 1126. Pan Guangdan, a Chinese historian, says that "the main group—the one which played the decisive role in obtaining approval for permanent residence and the construction of a synagogue and in establishing a regular religious life—most likely arrived during the Northern Song."[8]

Chen Yuan and Pan Guangdan, both of whom have studied the history at some length, believe that Jews settled in Kaifeng toward the end of the Northern Song dynasty, around fifty or sixty years before the capital was moved to Hangzhou. Their reasoning is not persuasive. A survey of temples in Kaifeng conducted in the middle years of the Northern Song does not mention a synagogue building. The two historians argue that the officials who conducted the survey would not have missed a synagogue if there had been one,[9] and therefore, since the presence of a synagogue indicates Jewish life, there were no Jews in the city at the time of the survey.

This is a fallacy based upon a misinterpretation of the survey's findings. The survey officials were counting buildings; they were looking for the structure of a temple, not the function of a temple. Their failure to find a synagogue building does not mean there was no Jewish religious activity in Kaifeng. According to the 1489 inscription, the city's Jews did not construct a building specifically for use as a synagogue until 1163, and most scholars accept this date. This explains why no synagogue building was mentioned in the survey. But the lack of a synagogue building does not mean that there was no Jewish community, and it certainly does not mean that there was no place for Jews to worship. Common experience verifies that newly arrived immigrants are unlikely to rush to build a house of worship in a totally strange environment. China, for this Jewish community, was an entirely different, probably alien, world. A good parallel can be found in the Tienjing Jewish community in modern China. Jews began to settle in Tienjing between 1860 and 1870 but did not construct a synagogue building until 1939, almost eighty years later. It would be a gross error to assume that the Tienjing community did not have a normal Jewish life during the intervening years.

The lack of a synagogue building does not mean there was no designated house of worship. While Jews need a place to assemble to pray in order to lead a normal Jewish life, no specific structure or fixed architectural pattern is essential. Unlike Christian churches, Muslim mosques, or Buddhist temples, all of which have rather specific physical requirements, almost any building will suffice for a Jewish service.

Thus it is neither surprising nor strange that the survey officials found no synagogue buildings in Kaifeng. They would certainly have failed to find a synagogue if their aim was to count temple-style buildings.

In addition, it is unlikely that Jews would have settled in Kaifeng in the early twelfth century because of the military and economic problems facing the Song dynasty at that time. Tartar tribes from Northwest China posed a constant threat of war. In 1126 during the reign of Emperor Kin Tsung, the Tartar army advanced to the walls of Kaifeng, and the city experienced the horror of invasion twice. In order to end a war he could not win, the Song emperor was compelled to accept extremely harsh surrender terms: "five million ounces of gold, fifty million ounces of silver, ten thousand oxen and the same number of horses, and one million pieces of silk."[10] To raise this immense indemnity, the court imposed levies on both rich and poor. "The rich were almost stripped of their wealth, and the houses of common people were invaded by the officers of the crown in their search for money."[11] Under these conditions, it was nearly impossible for people to make a living. It would have been even more difficult for newcomers. Had Jews come at this time, they would not have had the positive, good memories of the court and the city that are recounted in their own documents.

Therefore, it is more likely that Jews arrived in Kaifeng in the early Song. Gao Wangzhi, a Chinese scholar, dates the likely time as "by the end of the tenth century or the beginning of the eleventh century."[12] Of course, Gao is not the only one who holds this view. Donald Leslie also believes that the Jews came to Kaifeng "during the early part of the dynasty between 960 and 1126."[13]

In an article entitled "Some Questions Regarding the History of the Kaifeng Jews," Chen Changqi, another Chinese scholar, pins down the exact year when Jews arrived in Kaifeng and were, according to their traditional account, welcomed by an unidentified Song emperor. Chen says:

I believe that the "seng [monk] named Ni Wei-ne and others" who "arrived at our court from Xitian [the region west of China] . . . in the spring of the first month of the inaugural year of Emperor Zhen Zong," as stated in the History of the Song Dynasty, were none other than a rabbi named Levi and

a large group of Jews. Moreover, that the unnamed emperor
in the 1489 inscription was in fact Emperor Zhen Zong, and
988 was the unspecified time. The notation in the *History of
the Song Dynasty* is, therefore, an official record of the entry
of the Jews into Kaifeng.[14]

Chen's conclusion cannot be accepted without reservations, as it is
almost impossible to determine the exact year the Jews arrived. All
in all, it is likely that they came to Kaifeng during the early
Northern Song rather than the late Northern Song, especially if
we give credence to their own statements.

The Jews who came to Kaifeng in the early Northern Song may
not have intended to remain there at first. It was only after they
ascertained that the city was suitable for their business purposes
and comfort that they eventually moved from temporary to permanent status. As Pan perceptively notes: "Although they ultimately settled in China, it was not necessarily according to some
pre-arranged plan, but more a case of 'Since we're here, we might
as well stay.' "[15]

WHERE DID THEY COME FROM?

Several inscriptions left by the Kaifeng Jews imply that the community arrived directly from a foreign country. The inscriptions
give no hint that they might have come to Kaifeng from anywhere
else in China. Moreover, Jewish sources state that the first settlers
brought "entry tribute" with them when they arrived. This shows
that they were entering China for the first time. Otherwise it
would have been unnecessary for them to present entry tribute.

Is it possible that they lived in other Chinese cities before they
moved to Kaifeng? It does not seem likely, except in the sense that
the trek to Kaifeng may have been of long duration, so that they
stopped at various places along the way before reaching their final
destination. The welcoming words attributed to the emperor in the
1489 inscription, "You have come to our Central Plain [China];
honor and preserve the customs of your ancestors, and remain and

hand them down in Bianliang [Kaifeng]," read as if they were directed to newcomers to the imperial domain rather than to subjects who were simply moving from one part of it to another.[16]

According to Kaifeng Jewry's own account, their place of origin was called Tianzhu. This term occurs repeatedly in the inscriptions of 1489, 1663, and 1679. Its meaning is vague, but in modern Chinese Tianzhu normally refers to India. In other periods, it may simply have meant China's western region. Thus the term may only indicate the general direction of the Jews' place of origin. Many Chinese scholars who have studied the subject believe that Tianzhu designates an area much larger than India. For instance, Chen Yuan says:

> Tianzhu is an ancient term. As used here it simply represented a place far to the west. In the same way Adam is compared to Pangu. The purpose in both instances was to make the text comprehensible to people today. . . . So there was nothing wrong at the time in using Tianzhu to represent Judea.[17]

This is even more likely if one considers the limited knowledge of geography so many centuries ago.

In the 1512 inscription, the Kaifeng Jews added two Chinese characters, Xi-yu, which refer to the region west of China's western region, beyond Tianzhu. This can be seen as an indication that India may not have been their original home. Of course, the region west of the western region of China is a large area and could mean any country in the vast territory extending from Central Asia to Western Asia, i.e., the Near East.

Using the extant documents alone, it is impossible to pinpoint exactly where the Kaifeng Jews originated. Lacking documentary evidence that could throw light on the problem, one must turn elsewhere for clues.

An examination of the ritual books and other writings of Kaifeng Jewry may be of some help. Scholars who have studied this literature, largely created after the Jews settled in Kaifeng, find that quite a few words and phrases in their Hebrew prayers and their

Memorial Book are in Judeo-Persian. This points to Persia as a possible place of origin.

Cecil Roth, the great Anglo-Jewish historian, following a close examination of the Passover Haggadah of the Chinese Jews, points out "the extensive use made in it of the Persian language."[18] Herbert H. Paper, a scholar of Persian and a professor at the Hebrew Union College–Jewish Institute of Religion, says that "the Judeo-Persian [used in the Haggadah] is in the main accurate, well-written, clear, and 'normal.' "[19] Roth and Paper both "emphasize the fact that this ritual belongs to the Iraqi-Persian group of the Haggadah liturgy." [20]

Roth concludes:

The fact that the Chinese Jews used Persian in this fashion, as a sort of semi-sacred language, suggests that it was from Persia in all probability that they derived their origin, and certainly their religious teaching and inspiration during the course of their long, semi-isolated history.[21]

Since similar scraps of Judeo-Persian in Hebrew script have also been found in southern India, Afghanistan, Central Asia, and around the Red Sea and the Persian Gulf, further evidence is needed to decide whether the Kaifeng Jews were of Persian origin. Thanks to modern linguistic analysis, India is ruled out as the place of origin because the residual pattern of vowels used by the Kaifeng Jews is not associated with that used in India. As Norollah observes:

The pointings of the Persian words do not allow us to think that these colonists were of Indian origin at all; because one great peculiarity of the Indian pronunciation of Persian words consists in a broadening of sound, especially in the frequent use of "o" for "a," but this peculiarity is not to be observed in any of the MSS [manuscripts] in our possession.[22]

These considerations seem to be borne out by certain other indications. Therefore, Brotier might be right when he says, "They came from Hsiyu, which is the country of the West. It appears from all that can be got from them [the Judeo-Persian writings] that this Western country is Persia."[23]

The *Jewish Encyclopedia* agrees:

These books [of liturgy] . . . have been shown to belong to the geonic time [6th–11th cent.]—some of the piyyutim [liturgical poems] are compositions of Saadia [Saadia Gaon, 882–942]— and they were introduced into China from Persia. The ritual is decidedly Persian; and the directions for the prayers, the translations of parts of the piyyutim, as well as the colophons at the end of the Pentateuch sections, are in Persian.[24]

Leslie adds: "We may assume perhaps that when they arrived they followed the normal rabbinical laws and customs of Maimonides [1135–1204, the foremost medieval Jewish philosopher and legal authority], for their prayers are close to his."[25]

Rabinowitz states emphatically:

That the Jews of China came from Persia is undoubted, as there is a mass of corroborative evidence besides the facts already mentioned. There is first of all the liturgical evidence. . . . There is the evidence of their names. . . . Even a cursory examination . . . proves beyond question that many of the Hebrew names [of the Chinese Jews] are found only among Babylonian and Persian Jews. Thirdly, there is their own persistent tradition that they came from the West. And lastly, there is the evidence of a continuous contact throughout the succeeding centuries between these Jews and China. . . . The Chinese Jews of Kai-feng-fu are probably from Bokhara, the Persian rubrics in their liturgies being in the Bokharan dialect. The Bokhara Jews themselves have a tradition that their ancestors settled in various parts of Persia and especially at Salzawar, two days' journey from Meshed . . . and some of them emigrated thence to T'sheen Patsheen (China) but soon ceased to have communication with their mother-country, though they "carried their genealogies with them."[26]

The available information, though fragmentary, indicates beyond a reasonable doubt that Kaifeng Jewry was predominantly of Persian origin around the eleventh century. Perhaps we should add that while most of the Kaifeng community was originally from the Persian region, some elements might have had different backgrounds, as Pollak suggested, based on an examination of the textual and stylistic details of the Torah scrolls from Kaifeng.[27]

This may explain why the Kaifeng Jews had some traditions in common with the Jews of Yemen, and why they observed some of the customs laid down by Maimonides.

HOW DID THEY COME?

The Jewish written sources do not say anything about how Jews first arrived in the city. Legend says that they came by land—along the Silk Road.[28]

Was it possible for Jews to come to China by sea at that time? Sea routes between East and West were open long before the Song dynasty, and travel by sea was safer, cheaper, and easier than travel by land. Large numbers of merchants and traders from Persia or Arab countries were coming to China by sea during the Tang dynasty (618–907). They set out from the Red Sea or the Persian Gulf and crossed the Indian Ocean to the port cities along China's southeastern coast. This route is sometimes called the Sea Silk Road because its function was more or less like that of the Silk Road on land.

From the eighth to the thirteenth century, most of the trade between Europe and India or China was in the hands of Arabs and Persians. The main route was by sea from the Persian Gulf around India to Sumatra and Tongking, and as far as Canton, Quan-zhou, Hangzhou, and other Chinese ports. Jews were active in this trade, even though not noted for their seafaring prowess.[29] Pan says: "Sea routes between East and West were open during [the] Song [dynasty]. The Jews probably came with the Persian merchants from the Persian Gulf, across the Indian Ocean, to the various provinces of southeast China."[30] Zhu Jiang, another Chinese scholar, agrees.[31]

However, one cannot be certain. While it is true that many Jews, especially those who once lived in Quanzhou, Canton, Ningpo, and Yangzhou, arrived by sea, the Kaifeng Jews may have come by a different route. Quite possibly Jews who had come to China by the sea route subsequently joined the Kaifeng community. However, the core group of Kaifeng Jewry, the ones who played a decisive role in founding the community, most likely came by land. Traces of Jews in Dandan Uiliq, Dunghuang, and Ningxia, all of which are situated on the northern overland caravan route, serve as very strong evidence to prove this assumption.

As Leslie points out, most Jewish scholars favor the theory of the overland caravan route, in part because it fits in with what is known about the movement of Jews throughout Central Asia, including archaeological discoveries in Afghanistan and elsewhere.[32] In light of all this, and barring the discovery of reliable new sources that might warrant a reappraisal, it seems certain that the Silk Road was the route the Jews took to Kaifeng.

HISTORY

Kaifeng Jewry's continuous history of about nine hundred years is extraordinary in the annals of world Jewry. By and large, the history of Jews in the Diaspora is conditioned not only by their own heritage, tradition, adaptability, and cohesiveness, but also by the social environment of their country of residence. The development, growth, and fall of the Kaifeng Jewish community parallels in many ways the rise and decline of Chinese society and of the city of Kaifeng in particular. Therefore, we will occasionally examine major events and developments in the host society while recounting trends in the history of the Jews.

Development

The early period and formative stage of the Kaifeng Jewish community extended from the time of their arrival to the first half of the fourteenth century. Because the available records and documents from this period are few and far between, our knowledge about the early history of Kaifeng Jewry is limited. What we can surmise is that Chinese emperors permitted the Jews to remain in Kaifeng and to observe their own laws and customs, that they were allowed to acquire property and enjoy the same privileges as the native-born subjects of the dynasty, and that they adopted themselves very quickly and successfully in the new environment and lived peacefully and comfortably with the local people. Through their own efforts, they built up their homes and businesses and began to enjoy a secure and stable life. They had no need to worry about religious persecution because Chinese society is secular, and Chinese do not care what faith people practice and are tolerant of diversity. Therefore, the Jews were able to practice their religion freely.

The first few decades after their arrival must have been a good time for the Kaifeng Jews. As was noted in Chapter 1, the economy of the city was flourishing and business was excellent, providing many opportunities for merchants and traders. The Kaifeng Jews, as a part of the city's merchant class, must have benefited a great deal, which in turn made them feel comfortable about living in the city and becoming permanent residents.

Needless to say, the life of the Kaifeng Jews had its ups and downs. In the first half of the twelfth century, they must have suffered the same misfortunes as the rest of the city because of the wars between the Song court and the Tartars, who steadily gained in strength and in 1127 forced the Song emperors to abandon Kaifeng and move their capital to Hangzhou in East China. The suffering of the Jews as well as the city's native Chinese can be seen from the following account:

Beginning in the eleventh month of the previous year [1126], Jin (golden Tartar) troops besieged the capital for the second time, cutting the city off from the outside and depriving it of supplies of tribute and commercial grain, By the nineteenth of the twelfth month ". . . the price of rice in the city rose to

3,000 coppers per *duo* (peck), and the streets and lanes were littered with corpses of the starved." By the fourth month of 1127 the Jin army sacked the city, looting public and private property, and kidnapping Emperor Qin Zong and his father Hui Zong, as well as many other members of the royal family.[33]

During the early years of Southern Song (starting from 1127),

The New (Outer) City [of Kaifeng] was mostly in ruins. Some places had been converted into fields and put to the plough. In the Old (Inner) City a few markets lingered on. Here and there were tall edifices—the empty hulks of devastated palaces, pavilions and temples.[34]

No one knows exactly what happened to the Jews of the city. However, it would be surprising if they escaped the general suffering. Many of them probably died, and others left the city with the Song court, just as many Chinese did when Kaifeng was sacked and abandoned as the capital of the Song. The size of the population certainly dropped. The good old days of the Song court were etched in the memories of Kaifeng's Jews, as shown by their use of the Song calendar to mark the dedication of their first house of worship (which they constructed during the period of Tartar rule) when they recalled the event many years later in the fifteenth century.

However, those Jews who remained in Kaifeng were probably not mistreated by the new rulers. The Tartars, themselves a minority, also had a different way of life and thus must have been tolerant. When the Tartar rulers chose Kaifeng as their capital, the city was rebuilt. Its economy was soon back on track. The situation of the Jews improved greatly in the second half of the twelfth century, for they were able to buy a piece of land and obtain permission from the authorities to construct a synagogue, the first ever in Kaifeng. This event reveals that the community had not only recovered, but was somewhat prosperous.

According to their own records, the construction of the synagogue started in 1163 and was most likely completed in the same
year. This can be viewed as a part of the great effort to rebuild the
city after the Tartars made it their capital in 1127. We do not
know how big the synagogue was, but the erection of a house of
worship seems to testify that the Jews perceived their lives as more
secure and stable than before. No matter what the actual situation
was, we may surely say that the congregation had planted roots in
the soil of China by now: Kaifeng had become their home, and
the community had turned a new page, which prepared them to
lead a Jewish life in this strange world for the next seven hundred
years.

About a hundred years later, in 1279, the synagogue was rebuilt
on a larger scale with special permission from the authorities.[35]
From these two recorded events, both related to the synagogue, we
may assert that Jewish religious activity had become an accepted
part of the city's life.

Some scholars believe that during the Song dynasty, as during
the Tang, the Chinese government imposed a kind of extraterrito-
riality on foreigners. Special laws controlled relations between
Chinese and foreigners. Internal problems of the various minority
communities, including religious minorities like the Mazdeans,
Nestorians, and Manichaeans, were largely dealt with by the communal leaders according to their traditional laws. Foreigners found
it legally difficult, and sometimes prohibited, to own land or intermarry with Chinese. In some periods resident foreigners were segregated in ghettos. During the Yuan dynasty, which succeeded the
Song, the members of religious communities enjoyed a special
jurisdiction and some autonomy.[36] Perhaps this explains why Jews
in the early generations used their Hebrew names.[37] It was only
later that the members of the community adopted Chinese names.
The retention of their Hebrew names may also indicate that the
customs and traditions that made up their lifestyle were more
Jewish than Chinese.

From the thirteenth century on, China was ruled by the
Mongols, who established the Yuan dynasty (1279–1368). The

Mongols originated as pastoral horsemen on the steppes of what is now Mongolia. In 1206, under a leader named Chinggis (i.e., Genghis) Khan, meaning "ruler of the world," they went from conquest to conquest. Their domain soon extended from China over most of Asia into Russia and southeastern Europe. To administer this vast empire, they relied on their subject peoples and on foreigners.

Generally speaking, the Mongols distrusted the Chinese. They suspended the imperial examination system, which had been the traditional method of selecting government officials since the Tang dynasty. Instead, they utilized foreigners whenever possible. For instance, Marco Polo, a visitor from Italy, served the Mongol emperor Kublai Khan as an official for many years. Many Yuan documents show that the Mongols tried to impose their own way of life on their subjects. One Mongol decree prohibited Jewish and Muslim ritual slaughter because the emperor was offended when informed that members of these communities refused to eat meat from animals that they themselves had not killed. The emperor angrily exclaimed: "They are our slaves; how dare they not eat and drink what our court eats and drinks?"[38]

Aside from such incidents, however, the Mongols were not unfriendly to the Jews. They treated them like other minorities and allowed them to keep their own faith, engage in commerce and trade, and serve in the army. They also hired Jews as financial advisers and tax collectors.[39]

It is in the Mongol period that Chinese sources began to mention Jews, although not necessarily the Kaifeng Jews. The *Statutes of the Yuan*, for instance, cites a regulation issued on January 27, 1280, as stating: "Henceforward, Mussulmen [Muslims] and Jews, no matter who kills the meat, will eat it, and cease killing sheep by their own hands, and will cease the rite of *Sunnah*, such as the *namaz* (prayers) of five worships per day."[40] The *Official History of the Yuan* records a regulation issued on April 19, 1329, stating: "Buddhist and Taoist priests, Nestorians, Jews, and Ta-shih-man, who engage in trade, to be taxed according to the old regulation."[41]

On November 24, 1340, another regulation in the *Official History of the Yuan* states: "Ta-shih-man, Muslims, and Jews should be prohibited from marrying paternal cousins."[42]

It may be inferred from these documents that Jews and other aliens living in China still practiced their traditions and customs. The documents also indicate that Jews were visible in Chinese society to some degree.

As mentioned above, there is no evidence that the prohibitions enacted by the Mongols were directly aimed at the Kaifeng Jews. Most likely they were not. Nevertheless, Kaifeng Jewry must have felt their impact. One of the community's legends mentions that levirate marriage, a biblical practice whereby a surviving younger brother was required to marry the childless widow of his older brother, ceased in Kaifeng because of a Yuan decree prohibiting it.[43]

However, since the Mongols were too few in number to have a major influence on the mainstream, the ancient traditions and lifestyle of the majority of Chinese were not much changed under the Yuan. Nor did the Mongols much interfere with the life of the Kaifeng Jews.

Our knowledge about Kaifeng Jewry during the Yuan dynasty is quite limited, based as it is on just a few available materials. What we may say, however, is that Chinese traditions began to infiltrate their life during this period. Chinese culture, which has always emphasized the importance and continuity of tradition, made it possible for the Kaifeng Jews to preserve their traditional way of life. The concept of lineage, one of the strongest Chinese traditions, which traces common ancestry to a single person, had a powerful impact. The Chinese emphasis on clan bonds strengthened Jewish family values and family bonds, which in turn intensified the Jews' communal ties. History shows that lineage has provided stability to Chinese society for thousands of years. Integrated with Jewish values, it seems also to have contributed to the stability of the Kaifeng Jewish community for several centuries.

Irene Eber, an Israeli sinologist, observes:

The combination of family and sect identification was so firm that even if succeeding generations suffered increasing loss of remembrance, their Jewish past did not disintegrate, and was not erased from their memory. As a result of the specific process of absorption and adaptation that apparently began two hundred years after the arrival of Jews in Kaifeng, their sense of identity strengthened, was not sapped, in fact, persisted up until the twentieth century.[44]

We should add that newcomers may have joined the Kaifeng Jewish community during this period, especially in the Yuan era. It is a known fact that the Mongols invaded Central Asia and Europe in the thirteenth century and brought back many slaves, especially from Persia and the Arab countries, and surely some of them were Jews. After the captives were set free, some of the Jews among them may have settled in Kaifeng. A strong piece of evidence for the presence of newcomers is that the Kaifeng community's daily, Sabbath, and festival prayers resemble the liturgy of Maimonides and Yemen. These liturgical traditions, which had not been formulated in the period when Jews first came to Kaifeng, could only have been brought there by outsiders.

GOLDEN AGE

In the second half of the fourteenth century, Chinese society once again underwent a major change. The Mongols were overthrown, and the Han Chinese established the Ming dynasty (1368–1644). With the country's ethnic majority back in power, most Chinese were happier than they had been under the Mongols, especially as it mean that Confucianism and Chinese tradition regained their former place of dominance in society and people's lives.

During this period the Kaifeng Jewish community entered upon a kind of Golden Age. Unlike the Jews of Europe and the Middle East in the same period, they were encouraged to fully engage in the opportunities open to their neighbors, including public affairs and government service.

Already allied with the powerful feudal ruling class, the Jews involved themselves ever more in the city's commerce and learning. In 1390, they were granted land and additional privileges by Dai Zhong, the founder of the Ming dynasty. In 1421, permission was given by the emperor to rebuild the synagogue. In order to show their gratitude, the Jewish community placed an imperial tablet in the synagogue. In 1445, several new buildings were added to the synagogue compound, an indication that Kaifeng Jewry was prosperous and growing in size. In 1461, the synagogue was destroyed completely by a Yellow River flood, but it was fully restored by the community. In fact a Rear Hall was added to the new building, and outside a corridor connecting with the Front Hall. New Torah scrolls were obtained from Jewish communities in other Chinese cities, such as Ningbo and Yangzhou.[45]

The effort required for these communal concerns did not hinder Jewish achievements in Chinese officialdom, and in many ways the pace was accelerated. The number of Jews who passed the imperial examinations increased dramatically as time went on. According to Leslie, the 1489 inscription names thirty-two Jews, the 1512 inscription adds two new names, the 1663 inscription names thirty-three as active between 1642 and 1663, and the 1679 inscription adds five more names. All of these people played an important role in the community. The reverse side of the 1663 inscription carries a list of 241 names, "including 21 officials of the community and 38 civil, military, scholar, and medical officials in Chinese society."[46]

The 1489 inscription provides some insights into the center of this expanding Jewry. Its commercial activities were probably not solely local. As noted, the evidence shows Jews traveling to other cities on business. One example is the legend in which a Jewish merchant catches cholera while on a trip to a neighboring county to buy goods for the family business.[47] Connections with Jews in other Chinese cities, such as Ningbo, Ningxia, Yangzhou, and Hangzhou, seem to have been commercial as well as religious.

The Ming rulers were well disposed toward the Jewish minority and treated them equally. The Jews were apparently content with the situation, as can be seen from the statement about a Ming emperor in one of the synagogue inscriptions:

As soon as Emperor Kao, Dai-zhu, of our great Ming dynasty, had founded the dynasty, he first pacified the armies and peo-ple of the Empire. To all who responded to his beneficent influence, he bestowed land for settlement where they could live peacefully and happily follow their occupations. There was truly lack of favoritism and equal benevolence to all.[48]

The Ming dynasty was no doubt a turning point for the status of Jews in Chinese society. Around the beginning of the fifteenth century, a Kaifeng Jew by the name of An, a physician who served in the Honan Central Bodyguard Division, was promoted to assis-tant commissioner of the Embroidered Uniform Guard and assigned a new surname, Zhao, and given name, Cheng. Here is what the 1489 inscription says about him:

An Ch'eng, the physician, in the nineteenth year of Yung-lo (1421), by order of prince Ting of Chou, was given a present of incense, and permitted to rebuild the synagogue. In the synagogue was placed the Imperial Tablet of the Great Ming Emperor. In Yung-le 21 (1423), because he made a report to the throne and was adjudged meritorious for it, was granted by Imperial decree the surname Chao [Zhao], and the rank of a commissioner in the Embroidered Uniform Guard. He was promoted to be assistant commissioner of the Regional Military Commission in Chekiang.

According to Chinese sources, this honor was granted because he informed on the prince, who was residing in Kaifeng, although the Jewish source gives no hint of this.[49]

The significance of this event cannot be overemphasized. First, it shows that this Jew behaved righteously and with courage, and was loyal to his sovereign emperor. No wonder he received high honors from the emperor, including a new name. During the early

Ming period, aliens were not allowed to change their names, but the emperor changed the name of An Cheng (some scholars believe that his Hebrew name was Hassan)[50] to Zhao Cheng (meaning "Zhao the Honest" in Chinese). It was a court tradition to bestow honorific names as a reward for extraordinary service or achievements, and this was no doubt one of the greatest distinctions the Kaifeng Jews had ever received. As Pollak states, it was "a very meaningful concession to be given to a person of foreign extraction since, in the first part of the Ming dynasty, foreigners were not usually permitted to adopt Chinese patronymics."[51]

History shows that Jews most probably began to use Chinese names in the early Ming, especially after An San officially became Zhao Cheng. As Leslie notes, "The adoption of Chinese Surnames confirms both the assimilation and acceptance of the Jews by Chinese society."[52]

Not coincidentally, the Jew An was not the only member of the community to succeed in Chinese society. There were many such upwardly mobile successes. For instance, Kao Nien became a *Gong Sheng*, a title awarded for distinction in learning, and became an academic graduate in the Imperial College, during the Xuan-di period (1426–1436). After he passed the imperial exams, he was appointed district magistrate in She County of Anhui Province. Ai Chun of the Ai clan, another Kaifeng Jew, received the respected title of *Ju Ren*, which since the Tang dynasty had been bestowed on scholars who passed the imperial examinations at the provincial level. In 1447, he was appointed subdirector of studies in Sandong Province and administrator of the household of the prince of De.[53]

These achievements had much to do with the policy of the Ming dynasty toward the civil service examination system. The civil service system had been created to select government officials on the basis of merit. The tradition of recruiting talented people into the bureaucracy became a general practice during the Tang and Song dynasties. When the Mongols conquered China in the thirteenth century, the system was abandoned because they preferred to rely upon nonscholarly clerks who could more easily be controlled. After the Ming replaced the Mongols, the system was not only restored but refined. There were three levels of triennial examinations, and passing them all made one eligible for high office.

The measures taken by the Ming opened the political door for Jews along with everyone else. They provided a ladder by which Jews could rise in Chinese society. Success in the civil service examination system not only mean wealth, security, and recognition, but also may have "spark[ed] a Jewish mini-renaissance."[54]

It is not surprising that so many Jews flocked to enroll in Chinese schools, studied diligently, and prepared for the examinations. According to some reports, not more than one out of a thousand people who took the examinations would actually pass. Perhaps owing to their superior education and merit or to habits derived from the Jewish tradition of scriptural and talmudic study, the Kaifeng Jews earned promotion to official ranks out of all proportion to their numbers. At one time, it is estimated, more than thirty Jews passed imperial exams at different levels.[55]

In 1489, to mark the completion of the synagogue reconstruction, a stone monument was erected in the courtyard of the synagogue. The 1489 inscription was the first of a few highly valuable written documents left by the Kaifeng community and is the our main source for information about the community's early history.

From the inscription, we learn that the Kaifeng Jews had become Chinese in varying decrees insofar as dress, language, and mode of life are concerned, but still adhered strictly to their traditional religious rites and customs. In the sense that the community was prosperous and secure, that Jews did not live in isolation from the host society, and that religious life was thriving, we cannot fail to believe that the Kaifeng community had entered a Golden Age. Perhaps the strongest evidence is the attentive care for the synagogue, which was constantly repaired to keep it in a good condition. The record shows that the synagogue was rebuilt or renovated six times during the Ming dynasty.[56]

Moreover, consider the achievements of Kaifeng Jews during the Ming dynasty. More than twenty of them held degrees; fourteen served as court officials or military officers, and four were official physicians, one of whom served the prince directly. For one small community, this was indeed remarkable.[57]

All in all, the Kaifeng Jews in this period, especially in the six-teenth century, proved remarkably adaptable and enterprising. We have no doubt that all of them took Chinese surnames. Interestingly, enough, they only took certain surnames, and by the mid-seventeenth century only seven Chinese surnames remained in use: Zhao, Li, Ai, Gao, Jin, Shi, Zhang. Anyone who did not have one of these seven was not considered Jewish.[58] In addition, they spoke Chinese, wore Chinese style-clothes, and did many things in Chinese ways. They were not afraid of contacts with Chinese culture, and made creative use of Chinese wisdom and thought within the context of the Jewish faith. Perhaps the best example is their attitude toward ancestor worship, one of the fun-damental Chinese traditions.

So-called ancestor worship is the practice of making sacrifices to ancestors. The Chinese place food and burn incense before the ancestral tablets in the belief that the souls of the dead dwell there. It has been a rite of the Chinese for thousands of years, expressing the virtue of filial piety, and has nothing to do with idolatry. The basic function of ancestor worship is "to retain the cohesion and continuation of the family organization by using the memory image of departed kinsmen as an integrative symbol of perpetual kinship tie."[59] At its roots, ancestor worship has much to do with the lineage tradition which has been a structural core in tradition-al Chinese society.

Kaifeng Jewry set up halls for their own ancestors. The syna-gogue compound included an ancestral hall of the Li clan, an ancestral hall of the Zhao clan, the Hall of the Founder of the Religion in memory of Abraham, and the Hall of the Holy Patriarchs, in which incense bowls were maintained as tributes to the ancestors.[60] Gozani, a Jesuit missionary who had visited the Kaifeng Jews, described their ancestor worship as follows: "They honor their dead in the Tz'u-t'ang, or Hall of the ancestors, with the same ceremonies as are employed in China; but without tablets, they being forbidden the use of images and of everything of

that kind."[61] Ai Fusheng, a Jewish scholar in Kaifeng, also
described the practice:

> The spring sacrifices have to do with selecting and growing,
> and the autumn sacrifices with harvest thanksgiving, for we
> dare not forget the goodness of Heaven and Earth in the mat-
> ter of growth and harvest;
>   We reverence the ancestors in the temple, and sacrifice to
> the forefathers in the hall; by which also we express our desire
> to fulfill the offerings to the ancestors.[62]

Leslie believes that the Kaifeng Jews may have found it easy to
integrate such practices because of the similarity, at least superfi-
cially, between Chinese ancestor worship and the Yizkor and
Yahrzeit services for the dead.[63] The adaptation of this Chinese ritual certainly strengthened ties with the Chinese.[64] According to
Andrew Plaks, ancestor worship in the synagogue is best understood as an example of "creative cultural interaction rather than as
simple submission to the norms of the majority culture."[65]

Chinese imperial law required houses of worship to display a
tablet dedicated to the emperor. In feudalistic China, expressions
of loyalty and obedience to the emperor were very important. From
a Judaic perspective, the halakhic principle is that the law of the
land in which Jews live is binding upon them, so long as it does not
contravene halakhah.[66] The Kaifeng Jews emphasized this sort of
patriotism, and for a long time the community placed an imperial
tablet in honor of the Chinese emperor in its synagogue,[67] even
though it did not allow statues or images, which were forbidden by
the Ten Commandments.

The Kaifeng Jews may also have kowtowed to the imperial
tablet, a most extravagant act by which Chinese showed their
obeisance, and a dignified and admirable expression of respect.
However, to avoid the appearance of idolatry, the most important
prayer in Judaism, the Shema, was deliberately inscribed directly
above the imperial tablet. This marvelous and creative idea apparently indicated "that their allegiance to the One God they wor-

shipped took precedence over their allegiance to any earthly sovereign."[68]

Their creativity did not rest only on these rituals and rites. This period was also the time when Jewish scholars in Kaifeng were actively elaborating the doctrines of Judaism into a philosophical system in harmony with the current thought of the larger society in which they lived, much as Philo of Alexandria did in the first century, or Saadia Gaon in the sixth. In this line of endeavor, two Jewish scholars in Kaifeng, Zhao Yingcheng and Zhao Yingdou, wrote, respectively, *The Vicissitudes of the Holy Scriptures* and *Preface to Clarifying the Law*. Unfortunately, neither of these works has survived. Nowadays, we are able to see only the tip of the iceberg of their philosophic thought from the couplets they wrote to be hung in the synagogue.

The following samples provide us with a taste of the philosophic views of the Jewish thinkers of Kaifeng:

The Heavenly writings are fifty-three in number;
with our mouths we recite them,
and in our hearts we hold them fast,
praying that the Imperial domain may be firmly
established.

(by Ai Tien)

The sacred script has twenty-seven letters:
these we teach in our families and display on our
doors,
desiring that the Commonwealth may continually
prosper.

(by Ai Xiansheng)

Acknowledging heaven, earth, prince, parent, and teacher,
you are not far from the correct road to reason and virtue;
Cultivating the duties of benevolence, righteousness,
propriety, wisdom, and truth, you reach the first principles
of sages and philosophers.

(by Zhao Yingdou)

The Torah has its source in Heaven,
and the fifty-three sections record the facts concerning
the creation of Heaven, Earth and Man;
The religion is based on holiness,
and the twenty-seven letters are used to transmit the
mysteries of the mind, the way, and learning.

(by Ai Fusheng)[69]

These new philosophic expressions combined the wisdom and thought of Judaism and Confucianism. They demonstrated to the Chinese that the Jews openly admired Confucianism, showing the similarities, but also the differences, between it and Judaism. One reason they were able to make such use of these two ancient bodies of thought is explained by Kramer:

Judaism and Confucianism share certain basic tenets. Emphasis on filial piety is common to both, although with by far fewer ramifications in the Jewish than the Confucian structure of ideas. It would not be difficult, in a Chinese setting, to expand "Honor Thy father and thy mother" into the Five Relationships. In both systems, tradition wields tremendous influence. Obedience to a pre-ordained law or ritual or code is fundamental. In the case of Judaism, the Torah was established by the Supreme Deity. Although the concept of a Supreme Deity is absent from Confucianism, traditional beliefs receive the same respect as if they were God-ordained. They are further reinforced by governmental sanction.[70]

The Kaifeng Jews never hesitated to embrace elements of Chinese culture yet continued to adhere to their own faith. Their creative approach served as a model for the Jesuit missionaries who came to China in the seventeenth and eighteenth centuries.

This is illustrated by the conflict known as the Rites Controversy between the Jesuits, on the one hand, and the Franciscans and Dominicans, on the other. The dispute focused on the issue of what, if any, elements of Confucianism Chinese converts should be allowed to retain. While polygamy and polytheism, as practiced in Buddhism and Taoism, were strictly forbidden, Confucianist ancestor worship posed a more complex problem. Should it be condemned as idolatry or regarded as an essentially innocuous means of expressing reverence for one's ancestors, and therefore be tacitly, if reluctantly, permitted a place in the church?

The Jesuits argued that the Confucianist rite was purely secular and lacked theological content, as shown by the fact that the Jews of Kaifeng has adopted it in their house of worship. Clearly Confucianism was not a religion, they insisted, and if ancestor worship was acceptable to the Kaifeng Jews, who had so strong a belief in monotheism, then it should also be all right for Chinese Christians.

The Jesuits made a point of consulting the Kaifeng Jews about this problem. When Fr. Gozani asked about it, he was told that incense bowls were used but not tablets (except for specially honored members), and certainly not images.[71]

Fr. Matteo Ricci, the head of the Jesuit mission, agreed with this approach. He regarded most Confucian rituals as devoid of theology, asserting that they were social and civic practices. The Dominicans and Franciscans, however, held that Confucian beliefs and practices were incompatible with Christianity.

In 1643, the Congregation for the Propagation of the Faith condemned the Confucian rituals and warned that they were forbidden. The ruling offended Emperor Kang Xi, who retaliated in 1706 by ordering the Catholic priests in his empire either to continue the tolerant policy instituted by Ricci or leave the country.

This bitter dispute shook the foundations of the Roman Catholic Church and almost nullified its missionary program in the Far East. The banishment of the missionaries is important in the history of the Jews of Kaifeng because once the Christians were gone, all possibility of contact with Jews in other countries was also, and they returned to their former state of isolation.

Like Diaspora Jews elsewhere, the Kaifeng Jews were creative linguistically. Persian was most likely their mother tongue when they first came to the city, but there is no doubt that they picked up Chinese after a couple of generations. Of course, Hebrew, as a holy language, the language of ritual and prayer, was not abandoned and was still used for religious purposes and perhaps in daily life as well.

In other countries, Jews are known to have used Hebrew letters to write the local language and in time created unique new languages like Ladino (Judeo-Spanish), Yiddish (Judeo-German), and Judeo-Persian, each with its own rules and characteristics. The question of whether the Kaifeng Jews ever created a kind of Judeo-Chinese is, unfortunately, unanswerable. What we can say is that they definitely used the Hebrew alphabet to write out certain Chinese expressions and their Chinese names.

The best evidence for this phenomenon is the Memorial Book, dating from the seventeenth century, five or six hundred years after Jews first settled in Kaifeng. In it we find quite a few Chinese expressions written in Hebrew characters. For instance, the Chinese word for "eldest sister" is spelled *dalet zayin*, the Chinese for "second bother" is spelled *ayin sin*, and so on. The book transliterated the Chinese surnames used by the Kaifeng Jews into Hebrew characters. For example, Ai is transliterated as *ayin yud*, Jin as *gimel yud nun sofit*, Li as *lamed yud*, Shi as *shin alef*, Zhang as *gimel nun sofit*, and Tang as *tav nun sofit*. In addition, several given names are also written in Hebrew, such as Zhang Zhu-te, *gimel nun sofit / gimel nun sofit / dalet vav*; Jin Fu, *gimel yud nun sofit / peh vav alef*; and Zhao Liang-ching, *gimel mem lamed yud nun sofit / gimel yud mem sofit*.[72]

The social status of Kaifeng's Jews obviously had been elevated during this period, mostly due to their success in entering the ranks of officialdom. Their progress was most evident from the fifteenth to the seventeenth centuries, as attested by the titles of the Chinese who were associated with the community and involved in preparing the stelae of 1489, 1512, and 1663. In the fifteenth century, the non-Jews associated with the 1489 stele were only local scholars, baccalaureate graduates of *Lin-shan* grade.[73] In the sixteenth century, those who were associated with the 1512 stele were officials holding posts at the provincial level, recipients of doctoral degrees.[74] In the seventeenth century, those who were associated with the 1663 stele were either imperial ministers or imperial envoys at the state level.[75] This clearly demonstrates the community's rising social status. It must have earned considerable respect and approbation to have had imperial ministers and envoys as its friends.

The achievements of the Kaifeng Jews during this period won them a permanent place in Chinese society. They are now often mentioned in gazetteers, perhaps for the first time. For instance, the local gazetteers of Xiangfu, the district that constitutes the central city of Kaifeng, contain information about quite a few Jewish degree holders. Gazetteers from other parts of China record the distinctions of Kaifeng Jews posted to these areas. The provincial gazetteer of Kansu records a Kaifeng Jew as an army officer in 1900.[76] Around the end of the sixteenth century and into the seventeenth, Kaifeng Jewry produced its first family of renown, the Zhaos. Over the next hundred years, at least ten members of this family attained remarkable successes in Chinese society and played an important role in the community.[77] Their position in Chinese society may well have been an important factor in the Jewish community's enhanced status and prosperity.

As more and more Jews entered the ranks of Chinese officialdom, a new situation arose. Many brilliant men were forced to spend their best years away from Kaifeng because the government regulations prohibited officials from serving in their hometowns. Records show that quite a few Jews were assigned to posts in distant parts of China. For instance, Kao Nien, after passing the imperial examinations, was appointed district magistrate in She County of Anhui Province. Ai Jun was sent to Sandong Province.[78] Zhao Yingcheng was assigned to serve in faraway Fujian Province, in Huguang District.[79] "When on duty, a thousand or more miles away, he is a Confucian, responsible for Confucian education, possibly meeting no Jews."[80] This trend had a serious impact on the life of the Kaifeng Jews and contributed to their eventual assimilation.

Confucian education, in which one studied classical Chinese writings and nothing else, the only body of learning that guaranteed success in the civil service system, was a great force for acculturation and assimilation. While it provided capable Jews with access to high-status careers, it absorbed them into the larger culture and society, and impelled them to adopt Chinese cultural tastes and styles. This process conflicted with the traditional Bible-and-Talmud-based learning of the Jewish people. Without doubt, many of the community's most talented and ambitious members began to neglect the traditional Jewish curriculum in their effort to master the vocationally necessary Confucian canon.

The Chinese civil service system was so time-consuming that it inevitably entailed the abandonment of the study of Hebrew and any prospect of becoming learned in Judaism. Many Jewish scholars in Kaifeng, like Ai Tien, who spent almost all his time studying the Chinese classics, had little if any time to learn Hebrew. Religious studies were abandoned for the sake of success in the secular world. The negative effects for Jewish identity were obvious and serious.

Although the Ming empire was a mighty power, it was not much interested in the world beyond China. At the end of the reign of Yung-lo, it began to withdraw troops stationed outside the country. Voyages to faraway places ceased. The Ming government became more defensive and preoccupied with itself. During this period, as a consequence of the Ming policy both abroad and at home, Kaifeng became more and more provincial. After the Silk Road was abandoned around the fourteenth century, it had little contact with world trade routes and few contacts, if any, with Jewish communities outside China. In his discussion of the titles of the community's religious leaders, Leslie mentions that shaliach is somewhat problematic. This title literally means "emissary." It often designated a person who raised funds for Jewish institutions, but also was a title for the leader of the congregational prayer service. Several scholars have suggested that the Jews in Kaifeng who had this title may have been envoys to the community from Persia or Palestine.[81] If this could be proved to be true, then it would mean that the community had some (probably minimal) contacts with foreign Jews during this period.

What we do know is that Kaifeng remained in contact with other Jewish communities in China. In the fifteenth century, the Kaifeng Jewish community had frequent contacts with Jews in Ningpo, Hangzhou, Yangzhou, and Ningxia. For instance, in 1462 it obtained two Torah scrolls from Ningpo after its own were lost in a Yellow River flood. The Jews in Yangzhou helped to write the 1512 inscription and presented a Torah scroll to the Kaifeng Jews. While there is little evidence pertaining to the origin of the Jews in Ningbo and Yangzhou, we may assume that at least some of them moved from Kaifeng to those places for commercial or official purpose. Certainly this seems to have been so of the Jews in Hangzhou. A further discussion of this issue will be found in Chapter 6.

However, Kaifeng's contacts with these other Jewish communities would have ceased by the seventeenth century, when they vanished.[82] The Kaifeng Jews were now almost complete isolated. They must have yearned for an opportunity to reestablish ties with other Jewish communities, especially with the mainstream of its faith, to fulfill the Lord's commandment to keep in touch with one another and strengthen the bonds of brotherhood.

Many efforts were made. The best example can be seen in the the event that led to the European discovery of Kaifeng Jewry: Ai Tien's journey to Peking in 1605. The story of his meeting with the Jesuit Matteo Ricci has already been related in Chapter 1.[83] Ai's journey was a failure in that the foreigners in Peking were not Jews, but it made the world at large, and the European world in particular, aware for the first time of the existence of a Jewish community in China. Until this meeting, the Jews of Kaifeng had been totally unknown not only to Christians, but also to their fellow Jews in other countries.

Discussions of the Golden Age of the Kaifeng Jewish community often focus on its absorption into Chinese society. The trend cannot be denied, but it was a long, slow process. Preserving their Jewish identity was a prime concern of the Kaifeng Jews for many centuries. A close look at the actual way the community adopted Chinese names is an example. Leslie's list of Ai family given names, based on a thorough study of the community's Chinese-Hebrew Memorial Book, shows clearly that it was almost eight or nine generations before the Ai clan ceased using Hebrew names.

LIFE AFTER THE 1642 FLOOD

Two major events, one a local catastrophe, the other a national upheaval, heralded the end of Kaifeng Jewry's Golden Age. Both had far-reaching effects on the history of the community. The local event was the Yellow River flood in 1642, which completely destroyed the city of Kaifeng. The national event was a dynastic transition. The Ming dynasty, which had been in power for about three hundred years, was overthrown not by the peasant revolt that was directly responsible for the great flood in 1642, but by the Manchus, an ethnic group from Northeast China, who were invited to the capital to rescue the Ming emperor from the peasants. In 1644, the last Ming emperor committed suicide and a new Manchu dynasty, the Qing, was established.

The wild and turbulent waters of the Yellow River, a powerful stream sometimes called "China's sorrow," often overflowed. The flood of 1642, however, was not caused by nature but by human beings. The city had withstood a rebel siege for six months, but when it became apparent that it would not be able to hold out much longer, the governor of Kaifeng ordered the waters of the Yellow River unleashed in hopes of destroying the rebel army. The dikes were broken, but instead of hurting the rebels, the raging waters swept over the low-lying city, drowning a citizenry that was totally unprepared. From a population of 378,000, only a few score thousand survived.[84]

This was the worst flood the city had experienced since the fourth century, and Kaifeng was almost totally destroyed. More than half of its Jewish populace were killed, with only two hundred or so families managing to narrowly escape the deluge. The 1489 inscription states that there were seventy clans in the community and names seventeen of them. When the survivors were finally able to return to their homes after the flood, the number of clans had been reduced to seven: Li, Jin, Shi, Zhao, Gao, Ai, and Zhang. All the other clans were gone. When Ai Tien met Ricci, he mentioned that there were ten or twelve clans of Israelites in Kaifeng.[85] Wang Yisha, formerly the curator of the Kaifeng Municipal Museum, believes that some of the clans may have been wiped out in the flood, but that others never returned to the city and instead migrated to new homes in other parts of the country.[86] Whatever the reason, the local Jews now had only seven surnames. The community was never the same.

The Kaifeng Jews lost not only their homes and properties, but also their "House of the Lord." Most devastating of all, however, was the fate of their sacred scriptures, which were submerged beneath the waters covering the synagogue. As the Torah is indispensable to Jewish existence, the consequences of the loss of the holy books were dire, for it was unlikely that the community would be able to obtain new copies of the scripture when it was so isolated from contact with other Jews. Inspired by their rabbi, they rescued a few damaged texts and were able to copy them.[87]

In order to resume a normal religious life, the surviving Jews rented a large house on the north bank of the Yellow River, where they met for worship and daily prayers for about ten years.[88] When the time came, they eagerly returned to the city to rebuild their homes and businesses.

Fortunately the community had been on a very solid foundation both socially and financially before the flood. Thus its members could and did rebuild their lives and their synagogue. Much effort was expended in achieving this goal. They surveyed the site of the ruined synagogue to reproduce its original layout and dimensions, obtained official permission to rebuild the house of the Lord, and raised funds for the reconstruction.

All seven clans contributed money for the synagogue. Many individuals donated money to repair or recopy Torah scrolls. The project began in 1653, but it was ten years before the structure was completed and dedicated. The situation is reminiscent of the reconstruction of the Second Temple. The Kaifeng Jews' passion for their faith and tradition is underscored by the fact that the city itself was not rebuilt until ten years after they began the synagogue.

In 1663, a brand-new, magnificent synagogue compound was finally completed on the ancient site. Thirteen Torah scrolls were placed in the Ark. A grand celebration was held to honor the House of the Lord. A stone monument was erected to commemorate the event; this was the well-known 1663 inscription that provides so much detailed information about Kaifeng Jewry and its synagogue. The names of the community members recorded on this stele have helped later scholars to better understand the community. As Ezra and Sopher commented:

> It is affecting to think of this solitary stone continuing to bear its silent testimony after the synagogue has fallen, and the voice of its worshippers has ceased to be heard. . . . It deserves to be regarded as one of the most precious monuments of religious history.[89]

Another important communal endeavor during this period was the compilation of a Memorial Book. Written both in Hebrew and Chinese, this book listed the dead members of the community. Among other things, this document reveals that the community differentiated those who were and were not Jews by birth, especially the women. Each woman of non-Jewish origin is designated a "Daughter of Adam."

Why was the Memorial Book produced? Was it the first, or had there been similar books in the era before the flood? The 1663 inscription explained why the community was erecting a new monument: "Yet fearing that after a lapse of time this story would not be handed on, he desired to have it cut on stone to be transmitted to future generations." Could this have also been the reason the Memorial Book was compiled? Maybe the book was another sign that the community was beginning to worry about its future and that its history might someday be lost.

Kaifeng Jewry's struggle for survival is reflected in the effort to reproduce their Torah scrolls, most of which had been lost in the flood. Pollak's discussion of the scrolls may well serve as a description of the spirit of the community at the time.

. . . while the texts of the extant Chinese Torahs do exhibit some minor variations from the texts of the Torahs in common use today, these variations are the results of scribal lapses—and nothing more. The Pentateuch which the Chinese Jews knew was exactly the same as the one we know. The proliferation of scribal errors in the surviving Chinese scrolls becomes understandable when it is realized that at the time they were written the Jews of Kaifeng had already been cut off for at least a generation or two, and probably for several generations, from all contact with Jewish communities outside their country. In their isolation it was inevitable that the Kaifeng Jews should gradually become deficient in their knowledge of Hebrew. What is remarkable, really, is that the thousand or so Jews who lived in the city of Kaifeng . . . retained as much understanding of the language as they did.[90]

. . . the willingness of the amateur scribes of Kaifeng to attempt the rewriting of a dozen massive scrolls—a task probably requiring from six to twelve man-months of labor per scroll—and the readiness of the relatively small Jewish community, only a few years after it had suffered the ravages of war and flood, to provide the funds for a project of the magnitude (and to build a resplendent new synagogue as well) suggest that in the middle of the seventeenth century the ties of the Jews of Kaifeng to their ancient faith were still very much alive.[91]

The Kaifeng Jewish community continued to prosper despite the Yellow River disaster. Zhao Yingcheng, for instance, took the imperial examination in 1645, only three years after the flood, and passed it with the title of Jun Ren. A year later, he won the Jin Shi, the highest title ever received by a Kaifeng Jew, and was appointed surveillance vice-commissioner in Fujian and Huguang Provinces. His brother, Zhao Yingdou, achieved a similar honor soon after and served as a magistrate in Yunnan Province. In 1679, the Zhao clan erected an inscription in the Clan Hall.[92] Thus, despite the devastation and the reduction in size, the community's life was nearly back to normal.

The situation of Kaifeng Jewry in the early eighteenth century was described by two Jesuit missionaries, Gozani and Domenge, who visited the city. The found a small but flourishing community that still observed the festivals and held services on the Sabbath.

> They use truly Hebrew letters, which they learn to read from boyhood, and many even to write, as I have seen with my own eyes, both reading and writing; and whenever they write they use points to indicate vowels. They call the five books of the Torah or Pentateuch of Moses by their proper Hebrew names, *Berescith* for Genesis, and so on for the rest. In their conversation, they intermingle with the sacred books of Moses, the Pentateuch, many fables, which doubtless are derived from the tradition of the rabbinics of the Talmud. I am confident that some part of the Bible, especially a Hebrew version of the Pentateuch, might be obtained from them discreetly, and with not a little amount of money. They retain circumcision on the 8th day (after birth), the Passover, etc. They keep Sabbath day superstitiously to the extent that they do not ever light a fire of cooking food, which they must have cooked and prepared the day before.[93]

DECLINE

Although the Kaifeng community managed to rebuild its synagogue, signs of decline were emerging. Many causes can be cited: political, economical, and social.

A major change in China's political structure was underway. As mentioned above, the Ming dynasty, which had been in power for about three hundred years, was dramatically replaced by the Qing dynasty of the Manchus. The nationalistic Manchus were hostile to other ethnic groups. This is shown, among other things, by the imperial pronouncement of 1731 reminding local administrators that religion was not a proper consideration in the adjudication of

civil cases. Chinese officials in areas with substantial Muslim pop-
ulations had been making adverse decisions affecting Muslims on
the basis of their religion, a factor that eventually led to the widespread Muslim uprisings.[94]

The economic center of China was now further shifted to the
eastern coastal cities. As the overland trade routes diminished in
importance, Kaifeng and other inland cities gradually grew more
and more apart from the economic mainstream. Kaifeng became
no more than a provincial capital. Its size shrank. So did its economy and business.

The beginning of the eighteenth century also saw the growth of
tension and disputes between the Chinese government and the
Catholic Church, because the Qing rulers were becoming increasingly anti-Christian and anti-foreign. In 1704, in connection with
the Rites Controversy discussed earlier in this chapter, Pope
Clement XI issued a decree to prohibit Chinese Christians from
practicing Chinese rituals. This so annoyed Emperor Kang Xi that
the Chinese government began to expel missionaries from the
country.

The situation worsened with the accession of Emperor Yung-
cheng in 1723. To prevent missionaries from interfering in Chinese
affairs, the government once again decided to close its door to foreigners. In 1725, an imperial decree ordered all missionaries working among the Chinese to either go to Macao, an island colony on
the southern coast of China under Portuguese rule, or leave the
country.[95] In 1783, an order from the court dissolved the Society of
Jesus in China. Afterwards, the approximately eighteen hundred
Christian missionaries in China were often attacked and robbed.
The expulsion solidified China's isolation from the rest of the
world and thus had a profound implications for the Kaifeng Jews.
The expulsion of the Christian missionaries left them more alone
than ever, for the European priests had been their only contact
with the outside world. As Leslie says, "the Jews were now completely cut off from the Catholic missionaries, who we may suppose
gave them some encouragement after their links with Jewry had
been cut off earlier still."[96]

History finds China as a whole declining in the nineteenth century because of the closed-door policy of the Qing court plus numerous wars and invasions, not to mention natural disasters like floods and famines. There was a dramatic decrease in the country's population and a concomitant decline in the size of towns and cities. All of these trends took their toll in Kaifeng, and in 1841 so did another major Yellow River flood. In 1857, the army of the Taiping Uprising, a peasant rebellion against the Qing dynasty, marched on Kaifeng. To avoid the expected massacre, most of the city's residents, including its Jews, fled. Many of them never returned, which further reduced the size of the community. In 1860, another Yellow River flood struck the city. In its aftermath, the community's size was further reduced, and its economic status was further weakened. Maintaining a Jewish community requires a certain critical mass—a Jewish populace of a certain size and degree of prosperity. As the Kaifeng Jews became increasingly marginalized and impoverished, religious observances and communal identity suffered.

The Kaifeng community had long been cut off from co-religionists outside the country. Although Jews in Europe were persecuted and compelled to live in ghettos for many centuries, they could nevertheless communicate with other Jews, both for religious and commercial purposes, and could find successors to their deceased rabbis in case of need. The Kaifeng community was unable to do this, and thus its survival soon became problematic. As Stephen Sharot points out, "small numbers and lack of contact with other communities only made a community particularly susceptible to an absorbent environment."[97]

The political and social situation grew worse. Muslim rebellions broke out in the southwest (Yunnan Province) and the northwest (Shanxi, Gansu, and Chinese Turkestan) between 1855 and 1878, and were brutally suppressed. Since many Chinese regarded Muslims and Jews as more or less the same thing, the Kaifeng community began to fear for the first time that it might become the target of government action or mass hostility. The Muslim uprisings were followed by the Boxer Rebellion. The rebels particularly sought out foreigners and Christians. The Kaifeng Jews were frightened. To protect themselves from attack, they carefully and neatly chiseled their names off the memorial stelae that had stood in the synagogue compound for many hundreds of years. Gao Wangzi, a Chinese scholar, comments:

> Because it was Qing policy to suppress the Hui [Chinese Muslims] harshly, and because the Jews lived in close proximity to the Hui, they were often looked down upon. Some felt impelled to conceal their identity, and went as far as to obliterate their family names from those listed in the 1489 inscription. Racial oppression by the Qing government was the political cause of the disintegration of the Kaifeng Jewish community.[98]

Under the circumstances, Jewish life in Kaifeng underwent a radical change. The combination of floods, Taiping Uprising, and suppression of Muslims, like the straw that broke the camel's back, broke the community. Ezra and Sopher say that these events so completely ruined the community that the new generation was brought up in utter ignorance of everything connected with Judaism and the community's history.[99]

Unfortunately, we have very little information about developments in the Kaifeng Jewish community from 1723 to 1850, which Leslie calls "the lost century."[100]

The last account of a rabbi of the community comes from a sergeant in the Chinese imperial army named T'ieh Ting-an, who said that he had seen "the priest (who was an old man), walking round the temple followed by the people, and he carried something before him in his hands, like a cap, which he bowed over."[101]

A native of Kaifeng, T'ieh Ting-an lived for many years within a half-mile of the synagogue and was well acquainted with the Jews. In 1849, he told what he knew about the Kaifeng community to T. H. Layton, the British consul in Amoy:

> They are in all eight families, amounting probably to one thousand persons. Two families remain perfect. These are Kao

(High) and Shih (Stone). The head of the Shih family,
although he has forsaken the Jewish rites, has rebuilt the synagogue (perhaps repaired it). One of the family of Chin
(Gold) has been promoted by the Emperor to a high military
rank. Six families have intermarried with the Chinese. Two
families intermarry with Chinese Mohammedans only. The
Jews give their daughters to the Mohammedans; the
Mohammedans do not give their daughters to the Jews. The
Jews do not know from whence they came, or the period of
their coming into China. The Jews are quite Chinese in
appearance. The women exactly resemble the K'ai-feng
women. They have all straight features like the people in the
center of China. . . .

There are no priests; there is not any form of worship. One
rich man only takes charge of the synagogue. . . . No one Jew
can read or write Hebrew. . . . Some of the Jews say the sixth,
and some that the eighth day is their Sabbath (li-pai-jih).[102]

In the generations following the death of its last rabbi at the
beginning of the nineteenth century, Kaifeng Jewry seems, for the
first time, to have been unable to produce a leader capable of cop-
ing with the complicated spiritual and social tasks facing it. Nor
did a great preacher arise in its midst to evoke a creative religious
movement. No one was able to read the Hebrew Scriptures, and
before long services and rituals in the synagogue were neglected.
Without attendance the synagogue was under no one's care and
was eventually abandoned. Yellow River floods in 1841, 1849, and
1860 hastened the final destruction of the synagogue and the community's religious life.

Bishop George Smith of the London Society for Promoting
Christianity Among the Jews sent two Chinese Protestant converts from Shanghai to visit Kaifeng in 1850–51. They found the
synagogue in ruins and the Jews willing to sell their scrolls and
other manuscripts for a few silver coins. All told, the two missionaries bought six Torah scrolls and more than sixty Hebrew manuscripts in addition to the community's Memorial Book.

What a change from earlier centuries. In 1723, no matter what price was offered, the Kaifeng Jews refused to sell even a single Torah scroll. Earlier, they refused to even show the scrolls to Christians who had tried to convert them.[103] According to the Jesuit Domenge, they believed that "to sell the Torah is the same as to sell the God."[104] In 1851, a hundred or so years later, however, they were willing to sell them at any price, and by the end of the nineteenth century they had sold all their holy books.

Perhaps the city's remaining Jews sold the books because none of them could read Hebrew, or because the books no longer had value for them, or perhaps just because they needed money to survive. In any case, there had been a fundamental change.

Shortly before this, in a letter dated August 23, 1850, the Jews of Kaifeng asked Layton, the British consul, for help. Their letter reads like a desperate cry for assistance from a falling community. It is our chief source of first-hand information about the state of Kaifeng Jewry at this point near the end of its long history.

. . . during the past forty or fifty years, our religion has been but imperfectly transmitted, and although its canonical writings are still extant, there is none who understands so much as one word of them. It happens only that there yet survives an aged female of more than seventy years, who retains in her recollection the principal tenets of the faith. . . .

Our synagogue (ssu) in this place has long been without ministers; the four walls of its principal hall are greatly dilapidated, and the compartments of the hall of the holy men are in ruins. The ablution chamber and the repository (for the Scriptures) are in ruins likewise.[105]

The letter goes on to say:

We have now in the synagogue a map of the temple in T'ien-chu: at each of its nine gates are planted coloured standards; in the centre is a white jade stone, and in front are cotton trees. There is also a stream encircling the walls, near which are two large trees whose branches overhang the water. Daily at noon and midnight men climb the trees and cross the stream, in this way entering the temple for worship. This picture is preserved in our synagogue with great care. . . . An enumeration of individuals has not been kept, neither has any account been preserved of those who were separated from our community. . . . If much longer delay occur, not only will the synagogue (*ssu*) have fallen into ruin, but we fear that the holy books may likewise be injured by decay.

The subjoined are the names of persons who would mortgage or sell the synagogue buildings and materials: Chang china, Kao Mei-feng, and Kao Chin-yin (two brothers); Shih Sao-li and Chao Ning-te, have mortgaged portions of the building. Those who have pulled them down to sell are—Kao Puan, Kao Hsiao-te, and Chao Ta-chieh. If any person be deputed hither, measures should be taken to put a stop to the scandalous proceedings of these people.[106]

The two Chinese emissaries of the Anglican bishop of Victoria in Hong Kong, who traveled to Kaifeng and bought the holy books, reported:

We found [the synagogue] to be in ruins; within the precincts of the synagogue, were a number of small apartments, all inhabited by the descendants of the ancient people, who had spread out a great quantity of cabbages in the open air, just by the side of the synagogue. The residents there were mostly women.. . . . On asking them, "How many people live here and is the teacher still alive?", they said, "We who belong to this religion are the only people who live here, and our teacher is now no more; our temple is in ruins, and we are nearly stayed." We asked them, "Are there any who can read the Hebrew character?" and they said, "Formerly there were some who could, but now all have been scattered abroad, and there is none now who can read it."[107]

In 1866, when Martin, a Protestant missionary who hoped to convert the remaining Jews, visited Kaifeng, he found that the syn-agogue had vanished completely.[108]

J. L. Liebermann, a Jew from the West, paid a ten-day visit to Kaifeng in July 1867. He wrote to his father in Hebrew, reporting what he had seen and learned about the Jewish community, stating in part:

> Between the years 1840 and 1850, the synagogue was com-pletely ruined. Since then it had never been repaired, because the majority of those descendants of the Israelites are poor, and also because they do not feel the need of a synagogue, since they have forgotten the Law and its commandments. When the last of their elders died, the knowledge of the Scriptures completely ceased among them. By order of the government, scrolls of the Law were exhibited in the open market place, and an advertisement in Chinese was inscribed by the side, offering a reward and a leading position to any-one who would be able to explain the wording of the Scroll. Also the Jews made similar offers in other places, but to no avail. This caused them to despair of their synagogue, which was completely abandoned, and of which not one stone was left on the other. They were ordered not to adopt another religion before the arrival of persons who could read the Law, and who might re-introduce amongst them the knowledge now fallen into oblivion.
>
> I visited the site of their ancient synagogue and found nothing but stones, which were traces of the entrance-yard. . . . The stone lintel contained a Chinese inscription in large characters. The words were "li-fa su-sze Taou-kin-keaou" (which means "the House of God and the religion of those who extract the sinew from the flesh"). The place occupied by the synagogue is a wretched spot, covered with mire and pools of water. The majority of the Jews had become so entirely ignorant of their religion that they abandoned the tenets. Yet their descendants still abstained from eating swine

flesh and any meat killed by a stranger. They abstained from the use of blood, and the eating of anything impure of beasts, birds and fishes. They still had a burial-ground of their own.[109]

Liebermann's account is one of the finest descriptions of the Kaifeng Jewish community at the time.

The impoverishment of the Jews continued, and the number of poor increased. In former times, the tradition of charitable giving had bridged the gap between wealth and poverty, but now the gap narrowed. Perhaps it would be more accurate to say that wealth fell into far fewer hands, and thus the bulk of the Jews were all more or less unable to meet the great demands on their means: "There were beggars among the Kaifeng Jews."[110] The members of the community began to quarrel over the inheritance.[111] Some tried to sell the material of the synagogue, others the holy scriptures and Hebrew manuscripts.

Taking everything into consideration, the Kaifeng Jewish community ceased to function as a viable religious or collective entity in the second half of the nineteenth century, after the death of its last rabbi, the destruction of its unattended synagogue, and the sale of its holy books. Nonetheless, in 1912–14, Jews were still able to approach the local authorities as a group. The history of Kaifeng Jewry entered a new phase. While the Jewishness of the community was fading, a sense of identity lingered among those individuals whose consciousness would never let it die in their hearts.

Meanwhile, outsiders did not abandon all hope of rescuing the dying community. Quite a few efforts were made to revive Jewish life in Kaifeng. Jewish efforts to rescue the dying community began in the late nineteenth century. In 1869, for instance, the Protestant missionary Martin urged world Jewry to do its utmost to bring its Chinese co-religionists back to Judaism. "Nothing can save them from speedy extinction," he wrote, "except the re-building of their synagogue."[112]

But nothing had any effect or brought any result. Perhaps the most serious attempt was made in 1900 with the formation of the

Shanghai Society for the Rescue of the Chinese Jews. Its founders, most of them of Iraqi or Egyptian origin, were Jews who had come to Shanghai since the 1840s, when China was forced by its defeat in the Opium Wars to open its doors to foreign businessmen and companies.[113] On March 13, 1900, a letter signed by forty-six Shanghai Jews was sent to Kaifeng to express affection and support. It reads:

> Now, we assure you that we are eager to help you according to our ability, so that you may walk again in the footsteps of your forefathers. If you desire to rebuild the House of God, which has now become a wasted place, we will collect money and send it to you; if you want a teacher to instruct you, we will send you one; if it should please you to come hither and settle here in the city of Shanghai, we will help you to do so, and put you in the way to earn a livelihood by starting you in a trade, and all that you may require; in this city are men of our faith—great and wealthy men of affairs and business— who can help you to maintain yourselves and your sons and daughters.[114]

The intention and desire were genuine and sincere, but the effort was too slow, too little, and too late. Western Jewry was facing a severe situation that prevented it from taking an interest in Kaifeng: pogroms in Eastern Europe, and a seemingly endless flow of huge masses of poverty-stricken immigrants who had to be supported. Under these circumstances, the Jewish community of Kaifeng had practically no chance of recovery. Its few surviving members were totally impoverished. They could no longer form a nucleus for a possible reconstruction.

By the end of the nineteenth century all the holy scriptures and books were gone. In 1914, the site of the synagogue was finally sold by the Jews to the Canadian Anglican Mission headed by Bishop White. It is no exaggeration to say that by now the history of the Kaifeng Jewish community, which had existed proudly and distinctively since the eleventh century, was over.

However, individuals survived. Elements of Jewish tradition and identity are still apparent in the memories of some of the descendants of this once well-known and prestigious community. It is perhaps too early to say that the history of the Kaifeng Jews is completely ended. The new situation in China and the younger generations of the Jewish descendants may provide a new chance and perspective for the future. Let us recall Leslie's words:

Revival and renewal has accrued in the past elsewhere (e.g., the Bene Israel in India). The "rebirth" of Israel has produced a revival and strengthening of Jewish consciousness in many countries. Is it possible that the Chinese government will encourage such a revival to aid itself internationally? The recent "revival" of the Kaifeng Jews is surely linked to the Beijing government's recognition of Israel. The Chinese have an exaggerated view of Jewish importance in the world. A renewal of Judaism in Kaifeng is not impossible![115]

[1] The basic story of this legend was originally told by Zhao Pingyu, a Jewish descendant of the Kaifeng community, and collected by Wang Yisha, who published it in his *Spring and Autumn of the Chinese Jews*. The English version quoted here is from Xu Xin with Beverly Friend, *Legends of the Chinese Jews of Kaifeng*, pp. 1–2.

[2] It is so stated in the 1489 inscription; see below.

[3] Adler, *Chinese Jews*. See also Kublin, *Jews in Old China*, p. 99.

[4] Ibid.

[5] Domenge's letters of October 25, 1723 and December 20, 1724. Cf. Leslie, *Survival of the Chinese Jews*, p. 4.

[6] Kong Xianyi, "Delving into the Kaifeng Israelite Religion," pp. 5–13.

[7] Lawrence Kramer asserts: "The Kaifeng steles give three different dates of entry." See his "K'aifeng Jews," in Kublin, *Studies of the Chinese Jews*, p. 6.

[8] Pan Guangdan, *Jews in Ancient China*; in Shapiro, *Jews in Old China*, p. 54.

[9] Shapiro, *Jews in Old China*, p. 56.

[10] Li Ung Bing, *Outlines of Chinese History*, p. 188.

[11] Ibid.

[12] Gao Wangzi, "Assimilation of the Chinese Jews," p. 17.

[13] Leslie, *Chinese-Hebrew Memorial Book*, p. xx.

[14] Chen Changqi, "Some Questions Regarding the History of the Kaifeng Jews." In Shapiro, *Jews in Old China*, p. 142.

[15] Ibid., p. 54.

[16] Pollak, *Mandarins, Jews, and Missionaries*, p. 60.

[17] Shapiro, *Jews in Old China*, pp. 23–24.

[18] Drenger, *The Haggadah of the Chinese Jews*, p. 5.

[19] Ibid.

[20] Ibid.

[21] Ibid., p. 6.

[22] Norollah, "The Jews in China."

[23] White, *Chinese Jews*, pt. I, p. 52.

[24] *Jewish Encyclopedia*, vol. ?, p. 38.

[25] Leslie, *Survival of the Chinese Jews*, p. 24.

[26] Rabinowitz, *Jewish Merchant Adventurers*, pp. 73–75.

[27] Pollak, *Torah Scrolls of the Chinese Jews*, p. 90.

[28] Wang, *Spring and Autumn of the Chinese Jews*, p. 145.

[29] Leslie, "Kaifeng Jewish Community," p. 187.

[30] Shapiro, *Jews in Old China*, p. 32.

[31] Leslie, *Survival of the Chinese Jews*, pp. 21–22.

[32] Cf. Shapiro, *Jews in Old China*, pp. 115–116.

[33] Ibid., p. 116.

[34] The 1489 inscription.

[35] Leslie, "Integration, Assimilation and Survival of Minorities in China," p. 7

[36] The names of the first five generations of Kaifeng Jews registered in the Chinese-Hebrew Memorial Book are traditional Hebrew names. For details, refer to Leslie, *Chinese-Hebrew Memorial Book*.

[37] Leslie, *Survival of the Chinese Jews*, p. 14.

[38] Rossabi, "Muslims and Central Asian Revolts in Late Ming and Early Ch'ing."

[39] English version quoted from Leslie, *Survival of the Chinese Jews*, p. 14.

[40] English version quoted from ibid., p. 12.

[41] English version quoted from ibid., p. 12.

[42] Wang, *Spring and Autumn of the Chinese Jews*, p. 159.

[43] Eber, "Yehudei Kaifeng," p. 82.

[44] The 1489 inscription.

[45] Leslie, *Chinese-Hebrew Memorial Book*, p. xxxv.

[46] Wang, *Spring and Autumn of the Chinese Jews*, p. 157.

[47] The 1489 inscription.

[48] *Ming Veritable Records*, chap. 232. For details, see Chaoying Fang, "Notes on the Chinese Jews of Kaifeng." In Kublin, *Studies of the Chinese Jews*, pp. 87–90.

[49] For instance, Leslie says: "An San is almost certainly a transliteration of a foreign name such as Hassan." Cf. Leslie, *Survival of the Chinese Jews*, p. 26.

[50] Pollak, *Mandarins, Jews, and Missionaries*, p. 61.

[51] Leslie, *Chinese-Hebrew Memorial Book*, p. xxii.

[52] The 1489 inscription.

[53] Pollak, *Mandarins, Jews, and Missionaries*, p. 338.

[54] Leslie, "Integration, Assimilation and Survival of Minorities in China," p. 22.

[55] Leslie estimates that thirty-eight Jews passed the imperial examinations and became Chinese officials. Cf. Leslie, *Survival of the Chinese Jews*, p. 42.

[56] Based on the 1489, 1512, and 1663 inscriptions.

[57] Cf. Leslie, *Chinese-Hebrew Memorial Book*, p. xxxv.

[58] Wang, *Spring and Autumn of the Chinese Jews*, p. 46.

[59] Meskill, *Introduction to Chinese Civilization*, p. 646.

[60] The 1663 inscription.

[61] Leslie, *Survival of the Chinese Jews*, p. 88.

[62] White, *Chinese Jews*, pt. II, p. 149.

[63] Leslie, *Survival of the Chinese Jews*, p. 101.

[64] Two important problems facing the early Jesuit missionaries in China were the choice of a Chinese name for God and the rites performed to honor Confucius and familial ancestors. They found a model to follow in the creative applications of the Kaifeng Jews in these areas. For details, refer to Pollak, *Mandarins, Jews, and Missionaries*, and see also the discussion of the Rites Controversy below in this chapter.

[65] Plaks, "Confucianization of the Chinese Jews," p. 31.

[66] Katz, "Judaism of Kaifeng and Cochin," p. 132.

[67] The 1489 inscription mentions that the Kaifeng Jews had been placing such a tablet in the synagogue in honor of the emperor since 1423.

[68] Pollak, *Jews of Dynastic China*, p. 65.

[69] White, *Chinese Jews*, pt. II, pp. 149.

[70] Kramer, "K'aifeng Jews," p. 19.

[71] Leslie, *Survival of the Chinese Jews*, pp. 100–101.

[72] Leslie, *Survival of the Chinese Jews*, pp. 123–124.

[73] The 1489 inscription.

[74] The 1512 inscription.

[75] The 1663 inscription.

[76] For details, see Leslie, *Survival of the Chinese Jews*, p. 202.

[77] See T'ong Pao 53, nos. 1–3 (1967); Leslie, *Survival of the Chinese Jews*, pp. 147–179.

[78] The 1489 inscription.

[79] Leslie, "The K'aifeng Jew Chao Ying-ch'eng and His Family," p. 120.

[80] Leslie, "Integration, Assimilation and Survival of Minorities in China," p. 21.

[81] Leslie, *Survival of the Chinese Jews*, p. 95.

[82] Leslie, "K'aifeng Jew Chao Ying-ch'eng and His Family," p. 210.

[83] This account in chapter 1 is based on Ricci's reports and journal. Ai Tien reported to the community on his meeting with Ricci after he returned to Kaifeng. For further details, see Gallagher, *China in the Sixteenth Century*, p. 109.

[84] Wang, *Spring and Autumn of the Chinese Jews*, p. 41.

[85] Gallagher, *China in the Sixteenth Century*, p. 108.

[86] Wang, *Spring and Autumn of the Chinese Jews*, p. 43.

[87] The 1663 inscription.

[88] Ibid.

[89] Ezra and Sopher, *Chinese Jews*, p. 279.

[90] Pollak, *Torah Scrolls of the Chinese Jews*, pp. 20–21.

[91] Ibid., p. 114.

[92] This was the fourth inscription erected by members of the Zhao clan; it remained unknown until 1905, when it was found by Edward Jenks, who visited Kaifeng and met with some local Jews.

[93] Dehergne and Leslie, *Juifs de Chine*, p. 59.

[94] Broomhall, *Islam in China*, pp. 149–150. Cf. Leslie, *Survival of the Chinese Jews*, p. 173.

[95] Macao was occupied by the Portuguese in the sixteenth century. During the seventeenth and eighteenth centuries, it was an important base for missionary operations in China and in times of persecution became a place of refuge. Macao was returned to China in December 1999 under the same "one country–two systems" formula applied to Hong Kong when it was returned to China in July 1997.

[96] Dehergne and Leslie, *Juifs de Chine*, p. 13.

[97] Leslie, "Integration, Assimilation and Survival of Minorities in China," p. 20.

[98] Shapiro, *Jews in Old China*, p. 125.

[99] Ezra and Sopher, *Chinese Jews*, p. 262.

[100] Leslie, *Survival of the Chinese Jews*, p. 52.

[101] Ibid., p. 54.

[102] Ibid., pp. 53–54.

[103] White, *Chinese Jews*, pt. I, pp. 49–68.

[104] Dehergne and Leslie, *Juifs de Chine*, p. 147.

[105] White, *Chinese Jews*, pt. I, pp. 86–87.

[106] Ibid., pp. 88–89.

[107] Ibid., pp. 106–107.

[108] Ibid., pp. 184–187.

[109] Leslie, *Survival of the Chinese Jews*, p. 63.

[110] Wang Yisha, *Spring and Autumn of the Chinese Jews*, p. 231.

[111] Ibid., p. 220.

[112] Martin, "Jews in China," p. 5.

[113] For further information, see Leslie and Meyer, "Shanghai Society for the Rescue of the Chinese Jews."

[114] Adler, "Chinese Jews," pp. 116–117.

[115] Leslie, *Survival of the Chinese Jews*, pp. 32–33.

Chapter Three

The Inner Life of Kaifeng Jewry

THE KEHILLAH

The existence of an autonomous Jewish community, or Kehillah, was a universal feature of Jewish life in the Diaspora in premodern times. Based on principles of communal government developed in Babylonia and Persia in the talmudic era, the Kehillah was a tightly knit social unit that served both the general interests of the Jewish people and the self-interests and local needs of its members.

The Kehillah in Kaifeng was an organization of this kind. It served a dual function for its members, providing a forum for the assertion of Jewish identity and enabling them to enjoy a nearly totally Jewish life. Its functions included the establishment and maintenance of the synagogue and the supervision of such religious concerns as kosher meat, ritual baths, cemeteries, and charitable institutions.

The mode of life of the Jews of Kaifeng combined their Jewish heritage with elements derived from their Chinese environment. The Kaifeng community was patriarchal in nature, with families or an extended family circle as the basic unit, and several generations and often families sharing the same household.

The Size of the Kehillah

For the centuries with which we are most concerned, direct statistical information concerning the population of any city in China,

Kaifeng included, is almost completely lacking. Reliable statistical data are few and far between.

The Kaifeng Jews' own records, the 1489 inscription in particular, state that there were seventy clans when they first came to the city. It is hard to decide whether seventy clans means seventy families or seventy different family names, because in Chinese "clan" could mean both. However, the inscription lists only seventeen: Li, Yen, Ai, Gao, Mu. Zhao, Jin, Zhou, Zhang, Shi, Huang, Li, Nie, Jin, Zhang, Zuo, and Bei.[1] In any case, there were at least a couple of hundred Jews who came even if we take "clan" as meaning a family.

Another inscription (the one from 1679) says that "there were then 73 clans, more than 500 families altogether" when the community constructed its first synagogue in 1163. In this case, there would have been a few thousand Jews in the city. However, the figure is a pure guess, and most scholars do not think there were more than five hundred families in Kaifeng around 1163. Rudolf Loewenthal interprets the 1489 inscription to mean seventeen clans and seventy families, and sets a figure of 350 to 500 for the original group.[2] The figure of five hundred probably reflects conditions around the time when the inscription was composed in 1489. Therefore, it is reasonable to assume that the size of the community in the early years may have been anywhere between a few hundred and a thousand at maximum.

Population increased as time passed. The growth of the Jewish community in Kaifeng stemmed from two sources: immigration (mainly during the first half of this period) and natural growth.

Immigration came principally from other parts of China and from Central and Western Asia. One source of new residents may have been captives brought back by the Tartars and Mongols when they invaded Western Asia and Europe in the thirteenth and fourteenth centuries. Unfortunately, there is no solid evidence about the dispersion of these captives, among whom there were certainly some Jews.

Natural growth was probably the principal cause of the increase in population, although occasional newcomers may have some-

Table 1
Families listed in Kaifeng Memorial Book

Clan	Number of families
Ai	44
Zhang	14
Zhao	54
Jin	14
Kao	51
Li	52
Shi	12
Total:	241

Source: Leslie, *Survival of the Chinese Jews*, p. 109.

times joined the community. The principal factor governing population size in those centuries was the number of children surviving into adulthood rather than the level of the birthrate. Fragmentary empirical information on the Jews of Kaifeng indicates that more children survived to adulthood in affluent families than in poor ones. A number of genealogies show that business leaders, rabbis, and communal leaders had more children who reached adulthood. The Memorial Book supports this assumption.

On the other hand, natural disasters, famines, and wars were major factors that reduced population, especially the frequent flooding of the Yellow River. The major flood in 1642 destroyed the city of Kaifeng completely and reduced its population from 378,000 to less than 100,000.[3] More than two-thirds of the populace perished. Only around two hundred Jewish families managed to escape by crossing to the north bank, according to the 1663 inscription. Other floods also did great damage. After every flood, many Jews were forced to leave the city and go elsewhere for a more secure life. There were ten or twelve Jewish clans in Kaifeng before the flood of 1642.[4] Only seven remained afterwards. Some families obviously had left the city.[5]

As explained in Chapter 2, the Kaifeng Jewish community reached its cultural and economic peak—its Golden Age—in the seventeenth century. Did its population also peak at this time? Is it possible to estimate its size? To arrive at an answer, the period should be divided into two parts: before and after the 1642 flood.

Information about how big the community was after the flood provides a base for approximately determining the population before the flood.

Leslie believes that the numbers can be ascertained by thorough study of the Memorial Book of the Dead, a register in Hebrew and Chinese listing the deceased members of the Kaifeng Jewish community. When the book was closed in the 1670s (as Leslie believes), 241 Jewish families with seven different surnames were registered (see Table 1).

According to Leslie, there were 250–300 men, 200–250 wives, and perhaps 300 children (150 of each sex).[6] This number could have constituted about 200 family units, a figure confirmed by the 1663 inscription, which refers to about 200 families surviving the 1642 Yellow River flood. Thus it should be fairly reliable and presumably reflects the situation after the flood.

On the other hand, Leslie's list is by no means complete, because the Memorial Book does not include every member of the community. Nor was it a complete list of the deceased when it was compiled. For instance, it does not include any members of families with surnames other than the seven that appear in the book. Leslie himself recognized this, for he says:

> It is an incomplete lists of the dead of the community, because some several entries are by a different hand, some are added in the margins, others sprawling across corners; a few are circled (implying cancellation) or crossed out. The last page for each clan, in both the Register of Men and of Women, seems to have been added by a variety of hands.[7]

The difference is insignificant, and most scholars accept the number as is.

What about the population before the flood?

Wang Yisha, a Chinese scholar in Kaifeng, believes that there were more than five hundred families, about four or five thousand people altogether, before the flood.[8] "Calculating at eight persons to the average household in those days, that would be over four thousand people. Even at only five to a family, it would still be around three thousand."[9]

The community's population increase is reflected, at least indirectly, by the increase in the number of Torah scrolls it owned. Before 1461, there was only one scroll. Then two more were obtained from Ningbo.[10] The fourth scroll was probably brought in from Yangzhou at the beginning of the sixteenth century. Before the flood, there were thirteen Torah scrolls in the synagogue. The increase in the number of scrolls owned by the Kehillah certainly has some connection with an increase in population.

Wang's estimate is convincing. The survival of two hundred or so Jewish families after the flood actually confirms this. If we take into account the overall survival rate in the city (less than one-third), the total of Jewish families before the flood would have been more than five hundred, since the Jews would have suffered more or less the same losses in the disaster. Therefore, we may conclude that the Kaifeng Jewish community numbered around four or five thousand before the 1642 Yellow River flood. Certainly, this was the peak in its history.

Kramer takes much the same view:

If the Codex was indeed written in 1670, barely a generation after the terrible flood of 1642, which destroyed a large part of the population of Kaifeng, including a relative proportion of Jews, it seems illogical to assume that there were more Jews there twenty-eight years after the catastrophe then before. Therefore, if one accepts Laufer's estimate that the Jewish population of Kaifeng was approximately 1,000 in 1670, it must have been considerably larger before the flood, even if the initial settlement constituted less than 2,500.[11]

The Jesuit Gozani reported that there were "two or three thou-sand Jews" in Kaifeng in the early eighteenth century,[12] supporting the contention that the community had recovered from the disas-ter nearly a hundred years earlier. This number also agrees with general demographic trends in the area. "China's population grew from roughly 150 millions in 1700 to twice that a century later."[13] However, by the nineteenth century, there were no more than a few hundred members left in the Kehillah.

This dramatic drop in population resulted from more floods compounded by the sacking of the city during the Taiping Rebellion. Many were killed and others left. As the city's size and prosperity lessened, it became harder and harder to make a living there. According to Wang's survey, Jews of Kaifeng origin are scat-tered over fifty cities in China.[14] Wang's survey was conducted in the twentieth century and shows the current situation, but the movement of people it reflects began much earlier, most likely in the eighteenth and nineteenth centuries. Because of this, during the second half of the nineteenth century, the Jewish population of Kaifeng fell to several hundred, or even fewer, including children.

What about the population in the twentieth century?

From the survey conducted by Wang we learn that there were still 140 families of descendants of Kaifeng Jewry in China with six

Table 2
Jewish-descendant families in Kaifeng (1980)

Clan	No. of families	No. of persons*
Li	16	46
Zhao	9	11
Ai	17	32
Gao	3	3
Jin	2	7
Shi	32	67

*Men, 88; women, 67.

Source: Wang, *Spring and Autumn of the Chinese Jews*, p. 233.

surnames. Of these, seventy-nine families lived in Kaifeng, and sixty-one had moved to other parts of the country. At last count (1980) the seventy-nine families contained 166 persons, including thirty-six girls who had married non-Jews and left their parents' homes. However, this does not include Han and Hui girls who married into Jewish families. The breakdown according to surnames is shown in Table 2. Besides those who were living in Kaifeng, about the same number of Kaifeng Jewish descendants were scattered in some fifty counties of thirteen provinces.[15]

The Japanese invasion of China in the 1930s caused the most recent displacement of the Kaifeng Jews. According to Wang's account, the entire population of Kaifeng, before the Japanese army entered the city in 1938, was 327,949. Afterwards, only 127,949 remained (or according to some accounts, fewer than 100,000). Most of the residents fled to West or Southwest China to avoid a massacre by Japanese soldiers like the one in Nanjing around the end of 1937 when Japan captured the city.[16] The Jewish population certainly was reduced even further by these events.

Living Area

During the Song dynasty, when the Jews first arrived, Kaifeng consisted of three sectors: the Forbidden City, the Inner City, and the Outer City. Each sector was separated from the others by a wall. The Forbidden City was reserved for the emperor and his immediate family. Ordinary people were denied access to it, and even high-ranking officials were not allowed to enter without permission or invitation. The Inner City was chiefly for other members of the royal family and court officials and their families, as well as those who provided for their needs. Only the Outer City was for the general populace and for business. Poor people, however, could not afford to live there because housing was very expensive and rent exorbitant, so they resided on the city's outskirts. In general, foreigners were also not allowed to live there, and they too ended up in the suburbs. The place where the Jews lived was in

the eastern part of the Outer City, very close to one of the gates
leading to the Inner City, and they continued to live there until
modern times.

Unlike Jewish communities in Europe, the Kehillah of Kaifeng
was never segregated in a special quarter because of any formal
restriction by the host society. Nonetheless, throughout their history, the Jews of Kaifeng tended live in relatively close proximity
to one another. Earth Market Street, which is located in the eastern district of Kaifeng City, is believed to have been the place with
the heaviest concentration of Jews because it was very close to the
site of the synagogue. The location of the house of worship
remained constant, never changing even though the building was
rebuilt several times. It was convenient for Jews to live near the
synagogue, which was situated at the intersection of Earth Street
and Fire God Shrine Front Street, southwest of the Dawashi
Temple. The description in Ru Meng Lu, a Chinese book describ-
ing life in Kaifeng, says that the synagogue could be reached by
going from the Dawashi Temple to Earth Street, then eastward to
Li Family Lane.[17]

Earth Market Street could, therefore, be considered a Jewish
street, and the surrounding area could be conceived as the Jewish
quarter. Because of the large population of Jews, a side street in this
area was given a Jewish name, Tiao-Jin-Jiao Street, meaning
"Street of the Sect That Plucks Out the Sinews." Sometime around
the beginning of the twentieth century the name was changed to
Jiao-Jin Street, or "Teaching the Torah Lane," its current name.
This Jewish street did not differ from the city's other streets. It was
neither wider nor narrower, cleaner nor dirtier, roomier nor more
overcrowded than neighboring streets. The only difference is that
it was densely populated by Jews.

The houses in which the Jews lived over hundreds of years were
usually built of brick and tile, and in some cases had mud walls and
straw roofs. The layout of the houses was either a courtyard with
buildings on three sides or a few rows of chambers. A family of
three or four generations usually lived together. The interiors and
contents of the houses were apparently either similar to or identi-

cal with those of non-Jews except that there were no images and statues. Furniture was simple in those days. A heatable brick bed was essential because it provided a warm place in winter.

Of course, Jewish residence was never limited to this area, nor were non-Jews excluded. Some Jews preferred to live elsewhere in the city, and some Chinese chose to live in the Jewish area.

Based on the available information, the majority of the Jewish community always lived in the area around the synagogue. However, this changed after the loss of the synagogue and the disappearance of the community in the mid-nineteenth century. While a few Jewish families still lived there in the twentieth century, most were scattered throughout the city.

Administration

No existing document states straightforwardly whether or not the Kaifeng Jewish community had an administrative council to govern its daily affairs. However, the 1663 inscription lists the names of twenty-one communal officials who most likely formed a kind of governing body to take care of communal affairs and make decisions.[18] Among other things, it would have made rules concerning the maintenance of the synagogue, tax collection, and representation of the community to the Chinese authorities.

Unlike the Jewish communities in most European countries, which were usually headed by their wealthiest members, the leadership class of the Kaifeng Kehillah was probably made up of its most learned and educated men: rabbis, elders, and scholars who had passed the imperial examinations and been appointed as Chinese officials. The leaders were probably not elected, because election of officials was something very rare or even unheard of in China at that time. Those who became Chinese officials rose through a definite process; because of their status as court officials, they were widely respected and quite naturally would have their say in regard to communal matters. The higher they rose in officialdom, the more powerful or influential they would become. Since it was a Chinese tradition that officials also served as judges, it is possible that they joined the rabbis and elders in solving disputes and legal problems within the community.

The Kaifeng community probably did not have a Bet Din, a Jewish court that adjudicated disputes in accord with halakhah. The Jewish community had only limited autonomy and its self-governing procedures had to be acceptable to the Chinese government. However, the community did have the power to punish members for wrongdoings. For instance, the communal authorities were able to punish those who did not obey the laws of kashrut, and were even empowered to excommunicate members.[19]

The duties and functions of the council were not purely legislative. The communal officials were keenly conscious of their responsibility for maintaining a high standard of municipal honor and integrity. One of their most important duties was to represent the community in dealings with the Chinese authorities. For the benefit of the community, good relations had to be established with its neighbors and with officials at different levels of government, a goal that was usually achieved. Serving the community was a source of honor and prestige, as can be seen indirectly, if not directly, from the surviving inscriptions. The names carved on them are mainly those of officials who performed these functions.

The important role of scholars and Jews who were government officials in the administration of the Kaifeng Jewish community is due, first of all, to the fact that Jews were encouraged to participate in the Chinese civil service system and were appointed as officials if they passed the imperial examinations. This phenomenon also has much to do with the Chinese tradition of honoring scholarship more than business acumen. Merchants and traders were looked down upon, and their names were seldom noted in the official records even if they led exemplary lives. As a Chinese saying goes, "Everything else is low, learning [which leads to officialdom] is the only respected profession." Living in such a society, Jewish merchants and traders were not likely to occupy leadership positions in the community, even if their influence might be felt in other ways.

The frequent references on the stelae to those who contributed generously to the construction, renovation, and expansion of the synagogue may be taken, if one reads between the lines, as at least a partial enumeration of the wealthier members of the community, although some of these men were not necessarily the builders of the fortunes they possessed.[20]

In all probability the leadership of the community was composed of representatives of the different clans in rotation. This format would have satisfied the pattern of the governing organizations of Chinese communities at the time. According to Leslie, the 1663 inscription gives the names of twenty-one communal officials.[21] Perhaps they were leaders of the community at different times.

The Li clan, most likely descended from the tribe of Levi, apparently dominated the community's religious affairs. Twenty of the rabbis who served the Kaifeng Kehillah were from this clan.[22] The 1489 inscription mentions that the chief rabbi of the Kehillah was Lieh-wei of the Li clan. The 1663 inscription lists Li Chen as the chief rabbi who supervised the collating of the Torah scrolls retrieved from the floodwaters. A large percentage of the incumbents of the position of rabbi of the community came from this clan, clearly demonstrating that Li was an influential family. The Ai clan was another source of spiritual leaders. It produced a total of twenty-two rabbis.[23]

In the fifteenth century, the Jin clan (the Chinese character *jin* means "gold") seems to have held the foremost position in the Kehillah's leadership. The 1489 stele was erected by Jin Ying, and the text of the inscription was composed by Jin Zhong, both of whom were members of the clan.

From the seventeenth century on, members of the Zhao clan became the leaders of the community because of their achievements in the Chinese civil service. From Zhao Guanyu to Zhao Yingcheng, Zhao Yingdou, and Zhao Chengji, all played important roles in rebuilding the synagogue and reshaping the community after the Yellow River flood in 1642.

The rabbis of the community, especially the chief rabbi, definitely had authority. They were the leaders of the religion. Father Gozani described the chief rabbi as the "ruler of the synagogue."[24]

RELIGIOUS LIFE

Religious life was no doubt the most important part of the inner
life of Kaifeng Jewry before modern times. It was also the part of
their life we know the most about from their own documents. The
great devotion of the Kaifeng Jews to their religion can be seen
from the enthusiasm they showed in building, rebuilding, and renovating their house of worship.

Synagogue History and Structure

Jewish records state that the congregation began to build the synagogue in 1163. Prior to this, it may have rented a place as a house
of worship. The record says:

> In the kuei-wei year [1163], the 1st year of the Lung-hsing
> period of the Sung Emperor Hsiao, Lieh-wei, the Wu-ssu-ta
> [Ustad], let the religion, and An-tu-la [Abdullah] began
> building the temple. . . . It was situated Southeast of the Earth
> Market Street, and its four sides were each 35 chang [about
> 350 feet] in length.[25]

Presumably special permission to build the synagogue was
requested and granted.[26] The synagogue was rebuilt during the
reign of the Yuan emperor Kublai Khan in 1279. The name of the
synagogue is given as "Ancient Temple of Purity and Truth." Fang
Chao-ying points out the coincidence of these dates with the peaks
of foreign influence in China.[27]

> The next major reconstruction was in 1421, under the spon-
> sorship of the Prince of Zhou, posthumously called Ding, who
> was the younger brother of Ming emperor Chen Zu. During
> the Hong Wu period (1368–1399), he was appointed
> Governor of Kaifeng prefecture and had contacted the
> Kaifeng Jewish community. The third rebuilding was in 1445.
> The fourth was in 1461 after a flood. The fifth was in the

Cheng Hua period (1465–1488) when a Hall of Scriptures was added. The sixth was in 1489, which was the time of the first inscription. The seventh was in 1512, and the eighth in 1663, for both of which there were inscriptions. The synagogue was rebuilt for the ninth time in 1679. . . . The tenth and final rebuilding was in 1688, a fact attested to by many new vertical plaques.[28]

The synagogue was repaired or rebuilt at least nine times after 1163, based on Chen Yuan's account. The funds and efforts devoted to this were enormous. For instance, more than 100,000 gold pieces were spent for the construction of the synagogue in 1512.[29]

No doubt, the synagogue became the symbol of their identity and "always served as the focal point of the spiritual and communal life of the city's Jewish colony."[30] That is why each construction and dedication of the synagogue became so important an event in the history of the Kehillah. Because of its importance, several large stone columns were erected to mark the occasions. Much of what we know about the community comes from three of these columns: the 1489 stele, the 1512 stele, and the 1663 stele.

There has never been a fixed pattern of synagogue architecture, except for whatever is needed to satisfy the requirement that the worshipers face toward Jerusalem when praying, and generally such buildings reflect the styles of their time and place. The Kaifeng synagogue was no exception. The Chinese architectural influence was obvious and strong. It was a magnificent building with an ambitious design. One unique feature was its big-roof architecture, a distinctively Chinese feature.

The stele of 1489 mentions that the synagogue compound reconstructed in 1279 was about 35 to 40 chang (350 feet) long on each of its four sides.[31] No doubt the building within the compound was very large. We know the exact size of the synagogue that stood on the same site in the seventeenth and eighteenth centuries thanks to the stele of 1663 and the accounts (including both written descriptions and drawings) of Jesuits who visited in the eighteenth century.

The 1663 inscription states:

There were the Hall for the Holy Patriarch, 3 sections; the
Hall for the Patriarch of the Religion, 3 sections; North
Lecture Hall, 3 sections; south Lecture Hall, 3 sections; Great
Gateway, 3 sections; Second Gateway, 3 sections; kitchen, 3
sections; one Memorial Archway; Corridor, 9 sections; the
Imperial Tablet of the Ch'ing, in its dragon pavilion, set up in
the Hall; two pavilions for the inscribed stones; two shrines
for incense and devotion; and finally the painting in vermilion and the lacquering in black. . . . The pattern of the synagogue was finally completed, and compared with the former
one it was more complete.

The description of the synagogue compound by Finn is much more
elaborate and vivid, and deserves to be quoted at length:

The whole place of worship occupies a space of between three
and four hundred feet in length, by about one hundred and
fifty in breadth, comprising four successive courts, advancing
from the east to the synagogue itself at the extreme west.
    The first court has in its centre "a large, noble, and beau-
tiful arch" (*pae-fang*), bearing a golden inscription in
Chinese, dedicating the locality to the Creator and Preserver
of all things. There are also some trees interspersed.
    The second court is entered from the first, by a large gate
with two side doors, and two wickets beside them. Its walls
are flanked to the north and south by dwellings for the keep-
ers of the edifice.
    The third court has the same kinds of entrance from the
second as that has from the first. In its centre stands an arch
like that in the first court. Upon the walls, between trees, are
marble tablets (*Pae-wan*), with inscriptions in Chinese. Part
of this court is flanked by commemorative chapels: that on
the south, in memory of an Israelite mandarin named Chao,

the judge of a city of second degree, who formerly rebuilt the synagogue after its destruction by fire: that on the north, in memory of him who erected all the present edifice. There are also some reception rooms for guests.

The fourth court is parted in two by a row of trees. Half way along this line stands a great brazen vase for incense, at the sides of which are placed two figures of lions, upon marble pedestals; and at the westward sides of these lions are two large brazen vases, containing flowers. Adjoining the northern wall is a recess, in which the nerves and sinews are extracted from animals slain for food. The second division of this court is an empty space, with a "hall of ancestors" (*Tsootang*) at each of its sides to the north and south. In these they venerate, at the vernal and autumnal equinoxes, after the Chinese manner, but having merely the name of the person upon each tablet, without his picture. The only furniture there contained are a great number of censers; the largest one in honour of Abraham, and the rest, of Isaac, Jacob, the twelve sons of Jacob, Moses, Aaron, Joshua, Ezra, and others, both male and female. In the open space between these chapels, they erect their annual booths of boughs and flowers, at the Feast of Tabernacles.

Then occurs the synagogue itself, a building of about sixty feet by forty, covered by a four-fold and handsome roof, having a portico with a double row of four columns, and a balustrade before it.

Within this edifice, the roofs (as usual in Chinese domestic architecture) are sustained by rows of pillars besides the walls. In the centre of all is "the throne of Moses," a magnificent and elevated chair, with an embroidered cushion, upon which they place the book of the law while it is read. Over this a dome is suspended; and near it is the *wan-suy-pae*, or tablet, with the Emperor's name in golden characters, enclosed within a double line of scrollwork. This, however, is surmounted by the inscription, in Hebrew letters of gold:

HEAR, O, ISRAEL:
THE LORD OUR GOD IS ONE LORD.
BLESSED BE THE NAME
OF THE GLORY OF HIS KINGDOM
FOR EVER AND EVER.

After this, a triple arch bears the following inscription, likewise in Hebrew:

BLESSED BE THE LORD FOR EVER.
THE LORD IS GOD OF GODS, AND THE LORD:
A GREAT GOD, STRONG AND TERRIBLE.

Then a large table, upon which are placed six candelabra in one line, with a great vase for incense, having handles, and a tripod-stand, half-way along the line. These candelabra are in three different forms, and bear three different kinds of lights. Those nearest the vase bear torches, the next on each side have candles, and those at the extremities, ornamental lanterns. Near this table is a laver for washing hands.

Lastly, the Beth-el, or *Teen-tang* (house of heaven), square in outward shape, but rounded within. Into this none but the rabbi may enter during the time of prayer. Here, upon separate tables, stand twelve rolls of the Law, corresponding to the tribes of Israel, besides one in the center in honour of Moses, each enclosed in a tent of silken curtains. On the extreme western wall are the tablets of the Ten Commandments, in golden letters of Hebrew. Beside each of these tablets is a closet containing manuscript books, and in front of each closet, a table, bearing a vase and two candelabra.

The congregation when assembled for devotion are separated from the Beth-el by a balustrade, some standing in recesses along the walls. Against a column is suspended a calendar for the reading of the law.[32]

Father Domenge's sketch of the interior of the synagogue is very valuable, giving a clear picture of the layout and decoration of the inside of the house of worship. Father Gozani wrote the following description:

> I did not see any altar in it, there being only Moses's Pulpit, with an incense bowl, a long table, and some large candlesticks, with tallow-candles. Their synagogue bears some resemblance to our churches in Europe. 'Tis divided into three naves. The middle one is for the Table of Incense (offerings), Moses's Chair or Pulpit, and the *Wan-sui-p'ai* or Emperor's Tablet, with the tabernacles above-mentioned in which are preserved the thirteen copies of the *Sheng Ching*, or Pentateuch of Moses. These tabernacles are in the form of an ark, and the middle nave is as the choir of the synagogue. The two others are for praying and worshipping God. One may walk all round the synagogue, in the inside.[33]

The magnificence of the synagogue of Kaifeng Jewry can be better appreciated if it is compared with synagogues in India around the same period. For instance, the largest synagogue in Cochin in the 1600s was "thirty-five or forty feet in length and about one-third less in breadth."[34]

Synagogue buildings are important, but are only external evidence of religion. The internal evidence—what goes on in people's lives and practices—is far more important. Therefore, we need to examine the ritual life of Kaifeng Jewry in order to understand its religious life.

The Annual Liturgical Cycle

The rhythm of Jewish life, especially Jewish religious life, is regulated by the Jewish calendar. Though we do not have an actual calendar used by the Kaifeng Jewish community, observations by visitors tell us not only that the Kaifeng Jews must have had a Jewish calendar, but that they used it accurately. Kaifeng Jewry certainly seems to have observed the festivals on the correct dates. For instance, during his visit to Kaifeng in the early eighteenth century, Domenge, a missionary, was invited to participate in the service for Tabernacles. According to his records, the celebration took place on the twenty-third day of the eighth Chinese month, which was Saturday, October 3, 1722, or 22 Tishri 5483 on the Jewish calendar. This coincided with Shemini Azeret, the final day of the eight-day Tabernacles festival. Such evidence shows that the community "preserved most or all of the festivals and Sabbath services intact,"[35] as is confirmed by Bishop White in *The Jews in China*.[36]

If the Kaifeng community had a calendar, they must have made the necessary observations and calculations themselves. The Chinese calendar was not at all similar to the Jewish lunar-solar calendar, and therefore the Chinese among whom they lived would have been of no help in this area. This in itself is a good demonstration of the religious knowledge of Kaifeng's Jews during much of their history. Leslie checked the dates of all the festivals mentioned by Domenge and concluded that the Jewish calendar was being used, even though the days and months given were Chinese.[37]

In addition to keeping the Jewish calendar, the community publicly spelled out the rules for observing the Jewish holidays. For instance, the 1489 inscription clearly states that to observe Yom Kippur, the solemn Day of Atonement, Jews should

> close their doors for a whole day, and give themselves up to the cultivation of purity, and cut themselves off entirely from food and drink, in order to nourish the higher nature. On that day the scholar interrupts his reading and study; the farmer suspends his work of ploughing or reaping; the tradesman ceases to do business in the market; and the traveler stops on his way. Desires are forgotten, attainments are put aside, and all apply themselves to preserving the heart and nourishment of the mind, so that through direction there may be a restoration of goodness. In this wise it is hoped that while man remains at rest his heavenly nature will reach perfection, and his desire abating, his reasoning faculty will develop.

Similarly, the 1663 inscription says about the Sabbath: "The seventh day is specially for the cultivation of the virtues of purity and enlightenment. On the day of purification, food should not be cooked."

The holidays of Passover, Sukkot (Tabernacles), Purim, Simhat Torah, and Tisha b'Av were all observed. In 1722, Domenge attended Sukkot services in the synagogue and saw a sukkah hut in the synagogue compound.[38]

Kaifeng Jewry adopted a yearly circle for the reading of the Law, covering the whole of the Torah. The reading began with a special Maftir portion and was followed by prophetic portions. It is clear that these readings of the Law were very close to those known elsewhere.[39]

Here is a description of the ceremonial reading of the Torah reading compiled from the inscriptions:

First they washed their bodies, and changed their garments.[40]

Before performing acts of worship, he purifies himself and bathes, he dulls the ardor of sensual desire, he quietens his spirit, he adjusts his robes and his headdress, and adopts a dignified deportment.[41]

During the acts of worship the Law which is recited is sometimes chanted aloud, and in this the honouring of the Way is manifested. Sometimes there is silent prayer, and thus the Way is honoured in secret. . . . Advancing, the worshipper sees It in front of him; receding, It is suddenly behind him. Turning to the left, It seems to be to the left; turning to the right, It seems to be to the right.[42]

The congregation's religious devotion can also be seen from the respect given the rabbis. The names and merits of the rabbis are inscribed on the stelae. The 1489 inscription, for instance, says: ". . . thanks to their [the rabbis'] efforts, today all of our people observe the law, worship God, venerate their ancestors and are loyal to their sovereign and filial to their parents."

The prayers of the Kaifeng Jews included liturgies for daily and Sabbath worship, the Day of Atonement, New Year, Tabernacles, Passover, Pentecost, Purim, Hanukkah, and the Ninth of Av. They also included the recitation of Grace after meals, Kiddush, the Haggadah, and the Hazkarat Neshamot. There were special prayers and ceremonies for circumcisions, marriages, interments, and other events.[43]

In 1850, the Jews of Kaifeng still had all the Hebrew prayer books and Torah scrolls needed to conduct services for the festivals.[44]

The Kehillah of Kaifeng was unquestionably rabbinic in its outlook, but it is uncertain whether it actually owned a copy of the Talmud. In 1713, Gozani compiled a list that includes the titles of most of the talmudic tractates,[45] which may testify that it did have a Talmud. In any case, the prayer books that still survive indicate that the congregation's practice was in line with the traditions of rabbinic Judaism. In accordance with ancient practice, the Kaifeng Jews divided the Torah into fifty-three sections for an annual cycle of reading. According to A. Neubauer, their Grace followed the Sephardi ritual. There are certainly several variations associated with the Sephardi siddur (prayer book).[46]

Traditional religious culture is usually repetitive rather than innovative. Rituals, institutions, and norms of behavior in traditional societies are generally of value only if they are taken from exemplary models and imitate sanctified patterns. It is no different in Jewish tradition. But some small changes did take place, not perhaps in the norm so much as in the way the norm was construed in practice. Permissiveness usually prevails in new settlements, especially where little religious knowledge or learning finds its way in. This explains how and why the Kaifeng Jews adopted the Chinese custom of ancestor worship and built halls for their ancestors in the synagogue compound. As Kramer points out:

Judaism and Confucianism share certain basic tenets. Emphasis on filial piety is common to both, although with by far fewer ramifications in the Jewish than the Confucian structure of ideas. It would not be difficult, in a Chinese setting, to expand "Honor Thy father and Thy Mother" into the Five Relationships. In both systems, tradition wields tremendous influence. Obedience to a pre-ordained law or ritual or code is fundamental. In the case of Judaism, the Torah was established by the Supreme Deity. Although the concept of a Supreme Deity is absent from Confucianism, traditional beliefs receive the same respect as if they were God-ordained. They are further reinforced by governmental sanction.[47]

EDUCATION

The Kaifeng Kehillah, like all other Jewish communities, placed great emphasis on the value of learning. The traditional emphasis on learning may well have been strengthened by the fact that the Kaifeng Jews were cut off from Jewish communities outside of China. Without education, they would have been unable to practice their religion and maintain their heritage. To train their own "men learned in Torah" became critical and crucial, for they had to depend on these sages to guide them in prayer, instruct their children, and administer justice. Thus education served several functions for Kaifeng Jewry: it provided religious knowledge, especially to the children, and it raised up a cadre of leaders in each generation. In addition, and equally important, it enhanced their social status in Chinese society, which also greatly valued education and learning.

Rabbinical Education

We do not know very much about the details of Jewish education in Kaifeng, such as how teachers were selected, and whether the Kehillah had a talmudic academy, or yeshiva, or perhaps just a class for the few elite students who were expected to be rabbis when they grew up. Kaifeng had to train its own rabbis because the community could not hire rabbis from elsewhere. Of course, a place to study the Torah and holy scriptures was also provided for the lay members of the Kehillah.

The basis of the Jewish education of the Kaifeng Jews was most likely a knowledge of enough Hebrew to recite the prayers and the weekly Torah portion, as has been true worldwide, and the teaching of Hebrew seems to have been conducted orally from the older to the younger generation. The Hebrew knowledge of the Kaifeng Jews apparently varied over time, and as a result, the sources are contradictory. Some say that their Hebrew was poor in the seventeenth century;[48] others that their Hebrew was still good in the eighteenth century.[49] Their knowledge of Hebrew in the seventeenth century was at least good enough to conduct services, copy the Torah scroll, and write prayer books. However, they knew very little Hebrew in the nineteenth century after the last rabbi died. This may explain why they sold their Hebrew texts. In the twentieth century, none of them could read or write Hebrew.

A more extensive education was provided as part of the training for the rabbinate. We can see from the number of rabbis listed in the Memorial Book that rabbinical education was very active. In the seventy years from 1600 to 1670, eight rabbis were trained by the community. These included Rabbi Jacob, of the Li clan; the Master, representative (of the community), and teacher, Rabbi Shadai, of the Li clan; the representative, Rabbi Jeremiah, of the Li clan; the scribe, teacher, and representative, Rabbi Akiba, of the Ai clan; a scribe, Rabbi Mordecai, of the Kao clan; a scribe, Rabbi Judah, of the Shi clan; and a scribe, Rabbi Jacob, of the Kao clan.

Rabbi Jacob and Rabbi Shadai were father and son. Rabbi Jacob was the son of Rabbi Abishai, who was the son of Rabbi Eldad. Their family tree can be traced three more generations back in the Memorial Book (Nos. 343–350) to Rabbi Moses the physician.[50] All of them were members of the Li clan. Rabbi Jacob of the Li clan was the teacher as well as the representative of the community. Since the early rabbis of the community were mostly from the Li clan, we may assume that it was a tradition of the Li clan to serve in the synagogue. This supports the idea that the Li clan in Kaifeng was descended from the tribe of Levi, traditional priests serving in the Temple in Jerusalem before it was destroyed by the Romans in 70 C.E.

Ricci's report on the Kaifeng Jews in the early seventeenth century states that they received a fairly solid rabbinical education. He says that Ai Tien, the Kaifeng Jew who visited him in Beijing, was familiar with many biblical stories, including those of Abraham, Judith, and Mordecai and Esther. Moreover, by his own account Ai Tien knew much less than his brother.[51]

According to Ricci, the Kaifeng Jews' pronunciation of Hebrew was closer than his to the traditional Hebrew pronunciation. For instance, Ai Tien pronounced "Jerusalem" (*Yerushalayim*) as "Hierusoloim," and "Messiah" (*Moshiach*), who, he said, was still to come, as "Moscia." Ricci reports that Ai's brothers and many other Jews in Kaifeng also knew Hebrew.[52]

The Kaifeng Jews had not lost their knowledge of Hebrew in the eighteenth century, by which time they had been living in the city for more than six hundred consecutive years. Gozani wrote in his letter of August 25, 1712 that the Jews "start learning how to read Hebrew from childhood, and many of them also know how to write it; I have seen them reading and writing with my own eyes." They knew enough, in any event, to ask Gaubil to revolve certain grammatical problems they were having with the conjugation of verbs and the declension of nouns.[53]

The general level of Hebrew knowledge among the Kaifeng Jews was probably no lower than among Jews elsewhere, and most of the lay people seem to have been unable to understand any but the most familiar prayers. It was chiefly the father of the household who was responsible for the children's education, especially their Jewish education, since many of the mothers were not Jewish.

According to the 1663 inscription, Zhao Yingcheng wrote a book called *The Vicissitudes of the Holy Scriptures*. His brother Zhau Yingdou also wrote a work, *Preface to Clarifying the Law*, in ten chapters. These seem to have been works of biblical commentary. Had there been no rabbinical education in Kaifeng, these men would not have been able to write such books.

Secular Education

In the context of Kaifeng Jewry, secular education meant learning the Chinese classics in order to qualify for the civil service system, pass the imperial examinations, and rise in professional status. In China at large, the percentage of applicants who passed the examinations (as opposed to the total number who took them) was a mere one in a thousand. Even if we assume that the percentage of successful Jews was higher than the Chinese average, especially in light of the small size of the Jewish community, the fact that more than ten Kaifeng Jews passed the imperial examinations in the sixteenth and seventeenth centuries shows that a fairly large number of Jewish youth were involved in Chinese studies.

As Kramer observes, "Scholarship had no meaning unless the possessor of it succeeded in the examinations, and there was no chance of passing the examinations unless the candidate was schooled in the Confucian classics."[54] Thus many Kaifeng Jews must have sent their children to Chinese schools.

Let us take Ai Tien's family as an example to see the role of education in the Kaifeng Jewish community. Ai Tien's father was a well-to-do merchant in the sixteenth century. He had three sons. All of them were sent to school to learn how to read and write. Two studied rabbinical subjects and were apparently given as good a Jewish education as was available in Kaifeng. Both became rabbis, serving the community.[55]

The third son, Ai Tien, did not spend as much time as his two brothers on Jewish subjects and was not interested in learning to read Hebrew because he was attracted by the Chinese classics and aimed at a career in the civil service. He studied diligently and was a good student. He passed the imperial exams at the county level when he was only eighteen and became a Xiu Cai, the title given to junior scholars at the time. A few years later, he passed the imperial exams at the provincial level, received the respected degree title of Ju Ren, and was eventually appointed a county magistrate. Although he was ashamed of his limited Jewish education, as became apparent when Ricci asked him to read the Bible text, his strong devotion to Judaism is attested by the vertical tablet he wrote and contributed to the synagogue.[56]

The Zhaos are another example. In the seventeenth century, they became the community's leading clan. Zhao Chengji, Zhao Yingcheng, and Zhao Yingdou all passed the imperial exams and were appointed to official court posts. Their learning and status made it possible for them to play a major role in reshaping the community and rebuilding the synagogue after the destructive Yellow River flood in 1642.

Thanks to education, Jews were proportionally overrepresented in the local imperial examinations. Their success in the examinations, and their many outstanding achievements in Chinese society, particularly in the seventeenth century, testify to their thorough grounding in the Chinese classics.

At the same time they left a relatively rich Jewish literary heritage. They wrote their history and carved it in Chinese characters on a stele in 1489. They wrote many volumes of prayer books. Sixty-three prayer booklets were brought to the United States, and fifty-eight of them are now in the Klau Library of Hebrew Union College in Cincinnati. Perhaps the most valuable literary relic of the Kaifeng Jewish community is the Memorial Book, which is more than three hundred years old, and was written in both Chinese and Hebrew.

ECONOMIC LIFE AND OCCUPATIONS

The socioeconomic structure of the Jewish community of Kaifeng changed over the centuries. The first Jews to settle in Kaifeng were involved in the cotton and dying business. Many scholars believe that it was the cotton trade which initially brought Jews to China.[57] Jewish records mention that the first settlers took cotton cloth as a tribute gift to the Chinese emperor when they arrived in Kaifeng. Cotton fabrics were highly appreciated, because the cotton plant was not yet cultivated in China.

As time passed, the field of Jewish activities in Kaifeng broadened. Trade undoubtedly dominated at first, both on a large scale and local peddling. The documentary evidence for the first few hundred years is scanty and limited, but the mere fact that there was no discrimination against Jews opened the possibilities of professions and crafts. From the fifteenth century on, their trade routes led inland and locally rather than abroad and nationally. Jewish merchants dealt in many types of merchandise, including paint, textiles, and meat.

The 1512 inscription reveals that the members of the Kehillah pursued many different careers:

> Should one desire to see what is taking place today, it may be said that some, having gained degrees in literature, bring "glory to their parents" and acquire "renown for themselves"; and others, in positions of dignity either in or outside [the court], serve their prince and spread benefits among the people. Some are engaged in military operations, both offensive and defensive, and spend themselves in their loyalty and gratitude to the empire. There are those who cultivate moral qualities, and give an example by goodness to the whole country-side. Moreover there are farmers who till their fields in the country districts, and draw from the soil the wherewithal to pay the public tribute; and artisans who in their trades provide a sufficiency of articles of common use; and traders who are diligently engaged in commerce in far-away lands, so that their names are famous along the rivers and lakes; and finally, business men who are shopkeepers and make profits in the markets.

From this record, one can determine that some Kaifeng Jews were degree-holders, civil officials, military officers, and soldiers; others were professionals—physicians; still others were artisans— shoemakers, weavers, tailors, farmers. Of course, many were merchants and traders. Thus Jews were no doubt an integral part of the Kaifeng economy. Jews both manufactured and traded in jewelry. Jewish silversmiths owned shops in Kaifeng. According to a tale collected by Wang Yisha, a jewelry shop owned by the Shi family

manufactured a jeweled crown in a phoenix pattern that was presented by local officials to the Empress Dowager Cixi in 1901 when
she visited Kaifeng. She was so pleased that she rewarded the arti-
san generously.[58]

The traditional Jewish profession of medicine certainly
remained alive. Quite a few Kaifeng Jews practiced medicine and
some became well-know physicians. For instance, Ai Yingkui
became the official physician serving the prince of Zhou, a career
milestone that calls to mind Maimonides' post as court physician
in Egypt. Jin Yingshu was an ophthalmologist.[59]

The Memorial Book lists the names of five ritual butchers.
Understandably, ritual butchers were needed to supply kosher meat.

The report of Rev. W. A. P. Martin, who visited Kaifeng in 1866,
listed the occupations followed by the local Jews at that time:

> Some, indeed, true to their hereditary instincts, are employed
> in a small way in banking establishments (the first man I met
> was a money-changer); others keep fruit-stores and cake-
> shops, drive a business in old clothes, or pursue various hand-
> icrafts, while a few find employment in military service.[60]

Another report, by Ph. Berthelot, a French diplomat, in 1905,
provides some specific details about the occupations of individual
Kaifeng Jews based on their family names: Zhao was a tea-seller, Ai
a shoe seller, Kao a bricklayer, Li a soldier, and Shi the owner of a
silk mill.

Jews dealing in many types of merchandise peddled from door to
door. Trading between cities, despite the risk of robbery and con-
fiscation on the highways, was also carried on by Jewish merchants
as it was very profitable. Legends tell some of their stories.[61]

A report from the early 1900s says, "One of the family of Kao
kept a large spice and perfumery warehouse; and Shih (stone) has
a large silk shop. His name is Brown Jade Stone (Shih Tsung-
yu)."[62] This jibes with Wang Yisha's research. The silk shop mentioned in the report was very famous not only in Kaifeng, but in
Honan Province and nearby areas.[63]

Wang Yisha provides a list of the occupations pursued by Kaifeng Jews during the first half of the twentieth century:

7 proprietors of handicraft and mercantile shops, namely, the Wan Fu Silver Shop on Gu Lou Street, the Ji Feng Silver Shop on the same street, Shi Ziyu's Silk Emporium on North Local Products Street, a Money Exchange Shop, a Preserved Fruits Shop, a Restaurant, and a Wine Shop.
4 proprietors of goods and sundries shops
5 odds and ends dealers
2 independent handicraftsmen (one silversmith, one cotton flutter)
7 workers (3 house painters, 1 carpenter, 1 stevedore, 2 mailmen)
4 teachers (2 private school teachers, 1 family tutor, 1 missionary school teacher—female)
1 saltmaker and coaldust seller
1 vegetable peddler
1 bookkeeper in a foreign goods shop
1 Buddhist monk
1 unemployed[64]

This list is a good source for the Kaifeng Jewish descendants, but it does not reflect the situation hundreds of years ago.

Economically speaking, the Kaifeng Kehillah was well-off, especially during its Golden Age. Individuals were able to attain great wealth either through business or official status. For instance, three men paid for a substantial addition to the Rear Hall of the synagogue in the fifteenth century.[65] After the 1642 flood, several Jews who had become Chinese officials drew upon their personal incomes to fund the reconstruction of the synagogue.[66]

MARRIAGE

The centrality of the family is one of the most distinctive features of Jewish life and is thoroughly consistent with the place of the family in Chinese culture. The religious and ethnic unity of the family is an important element in its stability. Thus intermarriage has been discouraged since biblical times. In the fifth century B.C.E. it became so frequent that Ezra had to make it unlawful.

Kaifeng Jewry, like Jewish communities everywhere, tried to prevent intermarriages. According to an account written in the early eighteenth century, "They do not marry except among their own men and women. They admit no Chinese nor even Mohammedan into their Hebraic law, which, accordingly, they do not preach to others."[67] Other sources say the same. However, wishing is one thing; doing is another. Given the demographics of Jewish life in China, unions between Jews and native Chinese were inevitable. As Pollak explains:

> If they [the Jews] arrived essentially as traders—an inference which has been repeatedly drawn (though perhaps unjustifiably) by reason of the cotton they are thought to have presented to the emperor—then they presumably brought few or no women with them, and retained their identity only because, although they intermarried almost from the start, they were careful to hand down their Jewish loyalties to the children they fathered.[68]

By the early seventeenth century, intermarriage had been going on for generations. According to Ai Tien, many Jews in Kaifeng had "gentile wives and relatives." We learn from the names listed in the Memorial Book that intermarriage took place on a large, but not overwhelming, scale during the Ming dynasty. "Out of the women registered [in the book], over one quarter are 'daughters of Adam' of 47 non-Jewish surnames."[69] The rest were Jewish. Therefore, the majority of the community still married among themselves.

One should not assume that intermarriage between a Jew and a Chinese would bring an end to the family's Jewish life. It is a complicated matter.

First of all, the phenomenon of intermarriage in Kaifeng did not result from indifference to Jewishness but from demographic realities. The Kaifeng Jew who intermarried did so because he wished to marry rather than because he wished to intermarry.

Second, Chinese society is patriarchal. The family carries on the tradition of the father's side. Thus when a Jewish man married a Chinese woman, he was not assimilated into the non-Jewish world. The outcome was just the opposite: The non-Jewish female partner would be converted to Judaism or at least would follow Jewish rules in her daily life.

The custom for women to follow the rules of the husband's family was a deep-rooted Chinese tradition. As a Chinese saying puts it: "Follow the rule of chicken when you marry a chicken; and follow the rule of dog when you marry a dog." The stories and legends collected by Wang Yisha confirm that non-Jewish women adhered to Jewish customs and tradition after marrying a Jew.[70]

While this provided continuity when Jewish men married non-Jewish women, the same philosophy worked against Jewish identity for women who married out of the faith.

The children of Kaifeng Jewish women who married out would not have been regarded as Jewish because their mothers would have been obliged to follow the Chinese customs of their husbands, and they would have been raised as Chinese.

As a result, as Pollak observes, Jewish women who married out were permanently lost to the Kehillah, whereas Chinese women who married Jewish men were absorbed into it and thereafter counted as Jewish, presumably after a conversion ceremony.[71]

According to the records in the Memorial Book, Jews in Kaifeng had a wide range for seeking wives. The women of non-Jewish origin who married Jews came from almost fifty different clans of native Chinese.

Monogamy was the practice of most Jewish families in Kaifeng even though they did not know about Rabbenu Gershom ben Judah's ban on polygamy, enacted early in the eleventh century, and in any case would not have been bound by it because his ruling applied only to the Ashkenazi communities of Europe. Nonetheless, given the mores of feudal male-chauvinist China, polygamy was not nonexistent. In circles under the influence of the social practices of rich Han or Muslim Chinese, Jews might have had two or more wives or concubines. The Memorial Book notes that Zhang Mei from the Zhang clan, in the seventeenth century, had six wives, and that Jin Rong-Zhang from the Jin clan, in the eighteenth, had five.[72] In addition, Ai Qinyuin from the Ai clan, Li Qi-tang and Li Shao-tang from the Li clan, and Shi Qi-chang from the She clan each had two wives. Interestingly, according to Wang's survey, a good many Jews had more than one wife in the nineteenth century.[73]

The Kaifeng community maintained the practice of levirate marriage, whereby a man must marry his sister-in-law if his older brother, her husband, dies without fathering children. A legend stating that the Yuan emperor issued a decree outlawing this kind of marriage tells us indirectly that it was practiced, since otherwise the decree would have been pointless.[74]

In marriage, as well as in the other aspects of their lives, Chinese women were secondary and did not have much social standing, and this applied in many ways to the women of the Kaifeng Jewish community. Besides taking care of their families, the Kaifeng Jewish women helped in their husbands' businesses. Photos taken in the late nineteenth and early twentieth centuries show that Jewish women in Kaifeng bound their feet just as Chinese women did.

In feudal China, widows were not supposed to remarry. The Kaifeng Jews observed this rule. A woman called Gao, from a Kaifeng Jewish family, married Zhao Ying-fu, a Jewish man from the Zhao family. After her husband died, she never remarried, but instead mourned him for over forty years. She also devotedly cared for his mother and brought up their child single-handedly. Her virtue and high morality gained her great honor and won her a place in the Kaifeng gazetteer, which says: "Madame (née) Gao, wife of Chao Ying-fu, remained chaste and virtuous after he died for 44 years. She served her mother-in-law most filially, and looked after her orphaned child until he grew up."[75]

Wang Yisha explains why Jews in Kaifeng married girls with thirty-six different non-Jewish surnames during the Qing dynasty:

Shi Zhongyu, who works in the Bureau of Industry and
Commerce in the Shunhe district, and factory workers Zhao
Pingyu and Li Shichang, tell me that people of their great-
grandparents' generation married pretty much within the
seven Surnames. Li Shichang's great-grandmother was of the
Ai girl. The Shi clan and the Ai clan also intermarried with
one another.

But by their parents' and grand-parents' generations,
almost all married Han and Hui Chinese. This was due both
to the small numbers of their own race, and to their division
into rich and poor. Brides were no longer chosen on a racial
basis. It was rather a question of social status.

One ancestor of the Shi clan had been a Grade Four official, another a famous merchant—Shi Ziyu, who owned the
Bian (Kaifeng) Silk emporium. The clan had lots of property.
Its men selected their brides from clans of important scholars
or contributors to the Imperial Court. By the time of Shi Qi's
father, however, the clan was so down on its luck that he had
great difficulty in finding a bride.

Gao Fu's mother starved to death. His younger brother was
killed by Japanese soldiers. Before Liberation (1949) Gao Fu
lived from hand to mouth. It wasn't until after Liberation
that he was able to marry his present wife. Shi is not of Jewish
descent. As Gao puts it: "Among poor people, if the man and
woman suit each other they get married. Who cares about
race!"[76]

Wang did a survey of marriages of Jews in Kaifeng from 1851 to
the 1980s. He found that 22 percent of the Jewish women married
non-Jewish men, and that 84.6 percent of the women who married
Jewish men were of non-Jewish origin.[77]

FOODS/DIETARY LAWS

People in the region where Kaifeng is located lived mostly on
wheat-flour products, vegetables, a little meat, fish, and eggs. The

wealthy consumed considerable quantities of meat, fish, and wine. The Jews of Kaifeng ate more or less the same foods, but unlike the Chinese they observed kashrut, the dietary laws, and thus their meat was kosher, from ritually slaughtered animals.

The Kaifeng Jews had special foods for the Sabbath and for holidays. They ate fish on the Sabbath, and matzot and lamb for Passover. Gozani, in 1704, mentions the unleavened bread and paschal lamb.[78]

Zhao Pingyu, a Jewish descendant in Kaifeng, said that his family always ate matzot during Passover even in the twentieth century. The matzah he described is called *luobin*; it is an unleavened cake, flat, hard-baked, and made only of flour and water. "It is the bread of affliction," he explained. "It reminds us of the hasty way our ancestors left Egypt. They baked unleavened cakes from the dough which they brought out of Egypt. There was not sufficient time to leaven it, for they were driven out of Egypt and could not tarry."[79]

Another Passover symbol on the table was sweet mutton soup, equivalent to horseradish, with an unpleasant taste. Every member of the family had to drink the soup though it tasted awful. It served as a reminder of the bitter lives their ancestors led in Egypt, according to Shi Zhongyu, another Jewish descendent in Kaifeng.[80]

The dietary laws are one of the most unique practices differentiating Jews from other peoples. Dietary restrictions are not exclusive to Judaism. Most religions have norms for the feeding of the faithful. For instance, Islam prohibits pork and alcohol. Nevertheless, Judaism is much more detailed in this matter, because the precepts in the Bible, quite restrictive in themselves, have been expanded over the centuries by interpretation and practice. The laws of kashrut, in turn, have played an important part in other areas of Jewish life and custom. Certainly, kashrut was important to the Kaifeng Jews. The 1512 stele makes very clear that "in their meat and drink they are careful to observe the distinction between what is permitted and what is not."

To keep kosher, or try to keep kosher, is perhaps the longest-observed tradition of the Kaifeng Jews. Even today, their descendants do not eat pork, which is the main meat for the Chinese. Documentary evidence indicates that the dietary laws were care-fully observed, and that the communal authorities maintained strict religious discipline in this sphere. Ai Tien, the Kaifeng Jew who met Matteo Ricci in 1605, said that the chief rabbi had pro-hibited the members of the community from eating the meat of any animal not killed by his own hand.[81]

The strictness of Kaifeng Jewry's kashrut observance is evident from a popular saying among them recorded by Wang: "One is ousted from the community upon touching pork."[82]

In the early 1600s, when the Kaifeng community offered the position of chief rabbi to Father Ricci, the condition they set was that he "abstain from eating pork."[83] This is yet another indicator of how important the laws of kashrut were for the Jews of Kaifeng. In contrast, Ricci's belief that the Messiah had already come in the person of Jesus was regarded as a personal idiosyncrasy of little con-sequence.

Under the Jewish dietary laws, animals must be slaughtered and processed in accord with a series of complicated rules. The Memorial Book lists five men as Jewish ritual butchers around the seventeenth century. The skill was carefully handed down from generation to generation. There was a courtyard on the south side of the synagogue compound where the cattle were slaughtered according to the Jewish ritual and the prohibited sinews were extracted.[84]

Generally speaking, the dietary laws were carefully observed. "In all of these things they strive to take the Scriptures as their rule of conduct, and they hold them in veneration and believe in them with reverence."[85] Jews who became Chinese officials and were assigned to posts far away from Kaifeng may have deviated, and those who were invited to attend imperial banquets had to eat Chinese food.[87] Nonetheless, by and large the community was very attentive to matters of kashrut.

The community's adherence to the dietary laws is illustrated by one of the names applied to Kaifeng Jewry by the Chinese, *Tiao Jin Jiao*, "The Sect That Plucks Out the Sinews." The name reflects the fact that Jews, based on the story of Jacob wrestling with the angel in the Book of Genesis, are forbidden to eat the sinew of the sciatic nerve that runs in the hollow of the thigh. In accordance with this custom, the Kaifeng Jews always plucked out the sinew when they slaughtered an animal for food. The Kaifeng Jews never resented this Chinese name for their religion. In fact, they appreciated it because it differentiated them from their Muslim neighbors in Kaifeng, who also claimed Abraham and other biblical figures as patriarchs, and also abstained from pork.

A Kaifeng Jews told Ch'iu T'ien-sheng, a Chinese Protestant who was sent from Shanghai to visit Kaifeng Jewry, on December 10, 1850, that "everything that we eat, whether mutton, beef or fowl, must have the sinews taken out."[87]

In the second half of the nineteenth century, Fink discovered that "Jews now kept neither Sabbath, festivals not the commandment of circumcision, they, however, still abstained from eating swine's flesh or beasts not killed by them. They, moreover, still extract[ed] the veins from the flesh before eating it, nor did they eat blood or any other unclean things."[88]

Even today, Jewish descendants in Kaifeng still do not eat pork. It is interesting to compare the attitude toward the dietary laws in Reform Judaism. The Kaifeng Jewish descendants seem more authentic than Reform Jews in this respect.

CHARITY

The coherence of a Jewish community is shown by the solidarity of its members, manifested as charity to the poor and help for widows and orphans. We do not know the details of the welfare activities conducted by the Kaifeng Kehillah, but it certainly had machinery of some kind to alleviate the sufferings of its poorer members. Among other things, it collected and disbursed funds to relieve orphans and widows from want. It provided shelter as well, arranged marriages for orphans, and paid for funerals. The importance of aiding the needy was emphasized in the fifteenth century on a stele set up in the synagogue:

Concerning widows and widowers, and orphans and childless old men, and the lame and infirm of every sort, there is none that is not succored and relieved by compassion, so that no one becomes shelterless. If anyone through poverty is unable to arrange a marriage, or to carry out a necessary funeral ceremony, there is none but will hasten to bring him help, so that he may have the funds for a wedding, or the needed equipment for a funeral.[89]

Communal generosity must have been on a very high level, although the scarcity of sources makes it impossible to discover the full value of the donations by Jewish merchants and rich individuals. But it is known that in 1297 the Jin clan covered the entire cost of rebuilding the synagogue.

In the tenth year of the Zheng Tong period (1445), Li Rong and Li Liang used their own money to build the temple's Front Hall of three sections. Sixteen years later, a flood swept the entire synagogue away, leaving only the foundations. Li Rong again provided funds to build a brand-new temple "decorated with gilt and many colors." Other families also did their share. For example, members of the Gao Clan—Gao Jian, Gao Rui, and Gao Hong—paid for the rebuilding of the Rear Hall of three sections. Moreover, they provided funds to get three scrolls of the Torah and placed them in the synagogue.[90]

It was not only the rich who donated money; "all families contributed to the common fund."[91]

CLOTHING

In Christian and Islamic countries Jews were often required by law to wear clothing different from that worn by non-Jews, but the Jews of Kaifeng followed the fashions current in the general society. Their clothes were identical with those of their Chinese neighbors. To cite just one example, until the Chinese abandoned the custom of foot-binding, the Jewish women and girls of Kaifeng also had bound feet and wore the same tiny shoes as other Chinese girls and women. A drawing from the early eighteenth century and photos taken in the nineteenth and early twentieth centuries all prove this.

The only truly distinctive item of clothing worn by the Chinese Jews was a blue skullcap, which differentiated them from the Muslims, who wore white skullcaps. As will be discussed in Chapter 5, the blue cap was the basis for one of the Chinese names designating the Jews of Kaifeng.

CEMETERY/BURIAL SERVICES

In all probability, land for a cemetery was the first acquisition of Kaifeng Jewry, as of most new Jewish communities worldwide throughout history. The communal cemetery in Kaifeng was very old, and until the seventeenth century all of the Kehillah's dead members were buried in it. According to Wang Yisha, the communal cemetery was located either outside the West Gate of the city or in the northwest, near the village of Huasheng.[92] The layout of the cemetery was in "the direction of Jerusalem." A deceased Jew would be "shrouded in cloth, placed in a coffin, and buried."[93]

Unfortunately, the communal cemetery was destroyed in the 1642 flood of the Yellow River and was never reestablished. Instead, each clan purchased a separate burial place for its own members. These so-called family or private cemeteries were scattered in the suburbs of Kaifeng and came into wide use in the eighteenth century.[94]

Visitors are often surprised to find that there are no tombstones in the cemeteries of Jewish Kaifeng. This reflects Chinese burial custom. Only cemeteries for strangers have stone markers. To erect a stone in a family cemetery would imply that the members of the family did not know where their departed relatives were buried. The Kaifeng Jews followed this custom. Thus, the individual graves are unmarked mounds, although a nearby monument may give some general information.

According to the 1489 inscription, the burial ritual was Chinese, but Gozani reported in the early eighteenth century that the Jews still followed their traditional burial laws.[95] The Memorial Book includes the Kaddish prayer for the dead. Part of the text follows:

(a) May his great name be magnified and sanctified in the world (which he hath created according to his will); and in the world that he will create anew, where he will quicken the dead, and save the living; will rebuild the city of Jerusalem, and establish his holy temple; and will uproot all alien worship from the earth and restore the worship of Heaven to its place;

(b) For his name's sake, for his word's sake, and for the sake of the survivors of the exile, our brethren. May he remember us for our good, as in the days of old, may he bring near our end time, may he give (us) our Messiah, may he save us, and may he be gracious to our dead ones, in his comparison, during the lives of the sons of his temple, and during the life of all the exile of Israel,

(c) (even speedily?) and at a near time, and say ye, Amen.

(d) Let his great name be blessed for ever and to all eternity. Blessed, praised, and glorified, exalted, magnified and extolled, honoured and lauded be the name of the Holy One, blessed he; though he be high, high above all the blessings and hymns, praises and consolations, which are uttered in the world; and say ye, Amen.[96]

It seems quite likely that this prayer would have been recited at burial services.

[1] The 1489 inscription.
[2] Kramer, "K'aifeng Jews," p. 7.
[3] Wang, Spring and Autumn of the Chinese Jews, p. 41.
[4] Gallagher, China in the Sixteenth Century, p. 108.

5 Wang, *Spring and Autumn of the Chinese Jews*, p. 43.
6 Leslie, *Survival of the Chinese Jews*, p. 109.
7 Ibid., pp. 167–168.
8 Wang, *Spring and Autumn of the Chinese Jews*, p. 35.
9 Cf. Shapiro, *Jews in Old China*, p. 170.
10 The 1489 inscription.
11 Kramer, "K'aifeng Jews," p. 9.
12 Shapiro, *Jews in Old China*, p. 122.
13 *Encyclopedia of Asian History*, p. 306.
14 Wang, *Spring and Autumn of the Chinese Jews*, p. 233.
15 Ibid., p. 233.
16 Ibid., p. 237.
17 Leslie, *Survival of the Chinese Jews*, p. 84.
18 Ibid., p. 42.
19 Gallagher, *China in the Sixteenth Century*, p. 110.
20 Pollak, *Mandarins, Jews, and Missionaries*, p. 325.
21 Leslie, *Chinese-Hebrew Memorial Book*, p. xxv.
22 Ibid., p. 302.
23 For details, refer to Leslie, *Chinese-Hebrew Memorial Book*.
24 Ibid., p. 304.
25 The 1489 inscription.
26 Leslie, *Survival of the Chinese Jews*, p. 80.
27 Ibid.
28 Shapiro, *Jews in Old China*, pp. 40–41.
29 Gallagher, *China in the Sixteenth Century*, p. 108.
30 Pollak, *Mandarins, Jews, and Missionaries*, p. 274.
31 The 1489 inscription.
32 Finn, Jews in China, pp. 16–20.
33 Leslie, *Survival of the Chinese Jews*, p. 83.
34 Mendelssohn, *Jews of Asia*, p. 121.
35 Dehergne and Leslie, *Juifs de Chine*, p. 22.
36 White, *Chinese Jews*, pt. I, p. 75.
37 Leslie, *Survival of the Chinese Jews*, p. 89.
38 Dehergne and Leslie, *Juifs de Chine*, p. 22.
39 Leslie, *Survival of the Chinese Jews*, p. 91.
40 The 1489 inscription.

[41] The 1663 inscription.

[42] The 1663 inscription.

[43] Leslie, *Survival of the Chinese Jews*, p. 156.

[44] Ibid., p. 58.

[45] Leslie, "Kaifeng Jewish Community," p. 189.

[46] Marcus N. Adler writes: "One point is quite clear, that the ritual used by the Chinese Jews is identical with that laid down by Maimonides in the *Yad-hachazaka* [also known as the *Mishneh Torah*], which is also followed by the Yemen Jews. The Jewish colony may have followed a different ritual in olden times, but the ritual we find established during the last 300 years clearly came by way of Persia; all the rubrics, as Dr. Neubauer has clearly put it, are in the modern Persian language." Adler, "Chinese Jews," p. 109.

[47] Kramer, "K'aifeng Jews," p. 19.

[48] Gallagher, *China in the Sixteenth Century*, p. 34.

[49] Gozani's letter 1b, in Dehergne and Leslie, *Juifs de Chine*, pp. 58–60.

[50] Leslie, *Chinese-Hebrew Memorial Book*, p. 250.

[51] Gallagher, *China in the Sixteenth Century*, p. 108.

[52] Ibid.

[53] Pollak, *Mandarins, Jews, and Missionaries*, p. 108.

[54] Kramer, "K'aifeng Jews," p. 18.

[55] Gallagher, *China in the Sixteenth Century*; cf. Leslie, *Survival of the Chinese Jews*, p. 31.

[56] Ai Tien's vertical tablet reads: "The Heavenly writings are fifty-three in number, with our month we recite them, and in our hearts we hold them fast, praying that the Imperial domain may be firmly established." White, *Chinese Jews*, pt. II, p. 143.

[57] Laufer, "Chinese-Hebrew Manuscript," p. 164.

[58] Wang, *Spring and Autumn of the Chinese Jews*, p. 187.

[59] Leslie, *Chinese-Hebrew Memorial Book*, n.p.

[60] Leslie, *Survival of the Chinese Jews*, p. 61.

[61] See Wang, *Spring and Autumn of the Chinese Jews*, chap. 5.

[62] Leslie, *Survival of the Chinese Jews*, p. 54.

[63] Wang, *Spring and Autumn of the Chinese Jews*, p. 204.

[64] Shapiro, *Jews in Old China*, p. 173.

[65] White, *Chinese Jews*, pt. II, p. 13.

66 Ibid., pp. 64–65.

67 Leslie, *Survival of the Chinese Jews*, p. 105.

68 Ibid., p. 315.

69 Leslie, *Survival of the Chinese Jews*, p. 105.

70 Leslie's comment that "we must assume that these wives were adopted into the religion at marriage" seems sound and logical. *Survival of the Chinese Jews*, p. 105.

71 Pollak, *Mandarins, Jews, and Missionaries*, p. 316.

72 Wang Yisha, *Spring and Autumn of the Chinese Jews*, p. 96.

73 Ibid., pp. 71–137.

74 Ibid., pp. 151–161.

75 Leslie, "K'aifeng Jew Chao Ying-ch'eng and His Family," p. 131. It is indicative of the mindset of the time that the child is considered "orphaned" even though the mother is still alive.

76 Shapiro, *Jews in Old China*, p. 174.

77 Wang, *Spring and Autumn of the Chinese Jews*, p. 61.

78 Leslie, *Survival of the Chinese Jews*, p. 87.

79 Xu Xin, *Legends of the Chinese Jews of Kaifeng*, p. 136.

80 Ibid.

81 Gallagher, *China in the Sixteenth Century*; cf. Leslie, *Survival of the Chinese Jews*, p. 34.

82 Wang, *Spring and Autumn of the Chinese Jews*, p. 27.

83 Gallagher, *China in the Sixteenth Century*, p. 109.

84 White writes: "There was a slaughter house on the south, where animals required for food were killed by the synagogue authorities, in the prescribed way, which was no doubt the usual Kosher method." *Chinese Jews*, pt. I, p. 12.

85 The 1512 inscription.

86 Wang, *Spring and Autumn of the Chinese Jews*, p. 184.

87 White, *Chinese Jews*, pt. I, pp. 111–112.

88 Fink, "Jews in China."

89 The 1489 inscription.

90 Ibid.

91 Ibid.

92 Wang, *Spring and Autumn of the Chinese Jews*, p. 210.

93 Pollak, *Mandarins, Jews, and Missionaries*, p. 305.

[94] For details on the cemetery, see Wang, *Spring and Autumn of the Chinese Jews*, pp. 210–217.

[95] Pollak, *Mandarins, Jews, and Missionaries*, p. 96.

[96] Leslie, *Chinese-Hebrew Memorial Book*, pp. 10–12.

Chapter Four

Identity

The Kaifeng Jewish community had a consecutive history of about eight hundred years. By any account, it was the most dynamic, active, and important Jewish community in Chinese history.

The identity of the present-day Jewish descendants is often questioned because they look Chinese and seem to have entered fully into the variegated pattern of Chinese life. Moreover, the many reports and articles by Western visitors over the past three hundred or so years are often contradictory, especially regarding the faith and identity of the Kaifeng Jews. As a result, for a long time scholars doubted that the Kaifeng Jews really had much of an attachment to the Judaic heritage. Some believe that they were fully assimilated into the Chinese culture, and most especially Confucianism, by the seventeenth century. As Leslie comments,

> The terminology of the Chinese inscriptions from the synagogue is highly Confucian, with a few touches of Taoism. The ideas expressed are sometimes Jewish in Confucian garb, but more often Confucian per se. We hardly ever find passages from the Jewish Law translated into Chinese.

Looking into the religious life and faith of the Jews of Kaifeng after they migrated to China is by no means easy. This chapter will examine in some detail the attitudes, beliefs, and ritual practices that conditioned their identity, based on a analysis of the available documents. We will concentrate on the religious life of the com-

109

munity between the fifteenth and seventeenth centuries before
focusing on the identity of the Kaifeng Jews as individuals.

MEDIEVAL TIMES

The materials on which our examination is based are mainly writings by the Kaifeng Jews themselves that have survived the passage of time. These materials include the texts of the surviving
stone inscriptions dated 1489, 1512, 1663, and 1679, and some
veridical couplets, prayers, and other writings discovered in the
synagogue. The writings of missionaries who visited Kaifeng are
valuable and can serve as a reference, but we must deal with them
cautiously.

The German philosopher Immanuel Kant stated in 1790 that
when a body of people holding one faith enters the vast sea of
another, its own religion gradually diminishes until it is completely absorbed in the religion of the surrounding host. He singled out
the Jewish people, however, as an exception. Although they had
been isolated among alien religions worldwide for thousands of
years, they had managed to retain their faith intact.[2]

This is a complicated issue, especially when we are dealing with
Jews living in places where they were cut off from the rest of the world
for a long time and mixed harmoniously with their host society.

Benjamin Israel, an Indian Jewish scholar, addresses this issue in
relation to the Jewish communities of India, but his remarks apply
equally well to Chinese Jewry. As he points out, there is no such
thing as a "typically Jewish physiognomy" and Jews do not com-
prise a distinct race. Since ancient times, the adherents of Judaism
have always mixed with those among whom they lived, and thus
"it should be no matter of surprise for an Indian Jew to resemble in
many ways non-Jewish Indians rather than English or Russian
Jews."[3] Similarly, the external expression of Jewishness has always
been influenced by the customs and culture of the host society, so
much so that the observances of one group of Jews may appear
quite strange to members of another, and the pronunciation of
Hebrew too varies from region to region.[4]

The situation limned by Israel, in which loyalty to the ancestral religion and identity is combined with the influence of local custom is well illustrated by Kaifeng Jewry, as will be shown by the account that follows.

Let us begin with the synagogue. The intense Jewish commitment of the Kaifeng Jews can be seen in their enthusiasm for building or renovating their house of worship. The congregation constructed its first synagogue building in 1163, and in the years that followed repaired or rebuilt it at least ten times.[5] All of this required great effort and expense. The rebuilding described by Ai Tien, for instance, cost 10,000 ducats,[6] and it seems obvious that the community would not have made so huge an outlay if if did not value its house of worship.

The strong religious feeling of the Kaifeng Jews can also be seen from the name of their synagogue. It was originally called Qing Zhen Si ("Temple of Purity and Truth").[7] In time, the Muslims began using the same name to designate their mosques. During the 1512 renovation, to prevent the native Chinese from confusing the synagogue with a mosque, the Jews renamed it Zun Chong Dao Jing Si ("The Temple That Respects the Scriptures of the Way").[8] The new name shows that the Kaifeng Jews were eager to assert their separate religious identity.

The same strong feelings are revealed by their attitude toward their Torah scrolls and their strenuous efforts to reproduce them whenever the need arose. The best example is what happened when the disastrous flood of 1642 completely destroyed the synagogue. Shortly after the flood, a rescue operation began to save the sacred scrolls and other holy books stored in the synagogue. Gao Xuan, the eldest son of the Gao family (one of the seven well-known Jewish clans), entered the submerged synagogue several times to rescue scrolls. Later, all seven Jewish clans contributed time, money, and energy to the repair or reproduction of scrolls. The Zhao, Ai, and Gao families each repaired two scrolls, and the Jin, Shi, Li, and Zhang families were responsible for one apiece. Thus, all thirteen scrolls were reconstructed in a form as close as possible to their original condition.[9] As Pollak observes, it probably took from six to twelve man-months of labor to rewrite each scroll. The small Kaifeng community, faced with having to rebuild its homes and businesses after the flood, willingly undertook this difficult effort.[10] Surely there could be no better proof of its devotion to Judaism.

A full picture of the religious life of the Kaifeng Jews necessitates looking into how they understood their faith and heritage. The 1489 inscription recounts what they knew about the origin and the history of their ancestors:

> Abraham, the Patriarch who founded the religion of Israel, was of the nineteenth generation from P'an-ku Adam. From the creation of heaven and earth, the patriarchs handed down successively the traditions which they had received.

As for the genealogical transmission of the Jewish heritage, the 1512 inscription summarizes:

> From creation down, the Patriarch Adam handed it [the Torah] on to Noah; Noah to Abraham, Abraham to Isaac, Isaac to Jacob, Jacob to the Twelve Tribes, the Twelve Tribes to Moses, Moses to Aaron, Aaron to Joshua, Joshua to Ezra.

The 1663 inscription tells how Judaism began:

> Concerning the origin of the religion of Israel, it has come from a distant past. . . . Abraham comprehended the purpose of the union of Heaven and man, as well as the principles of moral cultivation and of human destiny. He knew also, that the Way of Heaven "has neither sound nor smell," and is very mysterious and profound, and that from it creatures are endowed with movement and with life, and are transformed and nourished in orderly manner. That is why he modeled no images, nor did he allow himself to be deluded by ghosts and spirits. He made the honoring of Heaven as the only principle, leading men to "develop completely their minds," and to

conform to Heaven, so that they could follow their minds and see the Way.

The 1489 inscription puts it another way:

> The Patriarch [Abraham] suddenly awakening as out of sleep, then understood these profound mysteries. He began truly to seek the Correct Religion [Cheng-chiao], with a view to assisting the true Heaven. With all his heart he served it, and gave himself up wholly to its respectful veneration. Then it was that he laid the foundation of the Religion which has been handed down to this day. On examination, it is found that this was in the 146th year of the Chou Dynasty [977 B.C.E.].

The inscription tells how Moses received the Scriptures from God at Mount Sinai:

> Through transmission (the religion) reached Moses, Patriarch of the Correct Religion. Examination reveals that he lived in the 613th year of the Chou Dynasty. From his birth he was gifted with a perspicacity that was pure and genuine. His benevolence and righteousness were altogether perfect; his principles and his goodness were together complete. He sought for the Scriptures at the top of Mount Sinai, and to this end he fasted forty days and nights. He put away his lustful passions, and denied himself both sleep and food, and with a sincere mind gave himself up to prayer. His devoted heart moved the heart of Heaven, so that the Law in fifty-three sections then had its origin.[11]

As for the uniqueness of Judaism, the tablet says:

> [The religion of Israel] makes no images, flatters no spirits and ghosts, and places no credence in superstitious practices. At any times the spirits and ghosts could not help men, idols

could afford them no protection, and superstitious practices could avail them nothing.[12]

And as for God:

Its presence is not impeded by visible form, its absence does not imply an empty void; for the Way is outside the limits of existence or non-existence.[13]

These statements clearly express the traditional understanding of the origins of Judaism, as well as the principles of monotheism and rejection of idol worship that are its basic tenets. The Chinese people—and this is a crucial point—never held any such ideas. In spirit and tone, these statements are completely Jewish, even if the language is Chinese. Since all the above passages were written between the fifteenth and seventeenth centuries, they can surely be read as reflecting the thought of Kaifeng Jewry at the time.

The Shema, the fundamental declaration of Jewish monotheism, is the first prayer taught to Jewish children and the valedictory uttered on the deathbed. This solemn declaration of faith, "Hear, O Israel, the Lord our God, the Lord is one," is recited as part of every synagogue service.

We learn from accounts by missionaries who visited the Kaifeng synagogue that the text of the Shema, inscribed in Hebrew letters, stood in full view of all the worshipers—emblazoned in gold and placed above the tablet set up in honor of the Chinese emperor. The implication is clear and obvious: Judaism, the faith of the congregants, superseded everything, including the emperor himself, whose presence in the synagogue was symbolized by the imperial tablet.[14]

The writings of the Kaifeng Jews open a window on their faith. Some scholars maintain that these writings were heavily influenced by Chinese culture, Confucianism in particular, and were inspired by and taken from Chinese teachings. Others hold that they were inspired by the Jewish spirit and express nothing but Judaism.

Even a cursory glance makes it obvious that the writings of the Kaifeng Jews are a mixture of Confucianism and Judaism. What is more, they use sayings taken directly or indirectly from Confucius and other Chinese classics. In order to better understand the linkage, it is necessary to briefly discuss Confucianism.

In the minds of many Westerners, Confucianism is a religion. However, those who have a deeper understanding of Chinese culture arrive at a different conclusion.

Confucianism does not involve a religious belief system. Unconcerned with deities, the spiritual, or what happens after death, it focuses on the establishment of a harmonious society, based upon a fixed idea of what each person's position and conduct demands—a society in which everyone does the right thing, especially in relations with others.

In the Confucian view, people can carry on proper relationships by adhering to the principles of mutual regard, duty, propriety, and wisdom. Where the Judeo-Christian religions see righteousness as striving to do the will of God, Confucianism teaches that the proper five relationships set up a peaceful social order. This is shown by its emphasis on the Chinese word *li*, which denotes ritual, protocol, and correct behavior, and centers on practice that is proper, correct, or permitted.

Thus Confucianism is a humanistic, rational, and secular worldview, a social ethic, a political ideology, a scholarly tradition, and a way of life, sometimes viewed as a philosophy. But to reiterate what was said above, it is not a religion. This is critically important for an understanding of why the Kaifeng Jews never hesitated to use Confucian sayings and customs in the synagogue. Since Confucianism has nothing to do with religious faith, they saw no conflict with Judaism.

It is interesting to compare the worship rituals of Kaifeng Jewry with those of Jews in other places. The 1489 inscription outlines the procedure to be followed in the ceremonial act of venerating God:

At first, the worshipper bends his body to honor the God, and the God is present in the act of bending the body. Then he stands erect, without leaning, to honor the God, and the God is present in the act of standing erect. In response, he preserves his quietude of mind, and by silent praise he honors the God, for that which should not be forgotten is Heaven. In movement, he examines his conduct, and by vocal praise he honors the Way, for that which should not be substituted for is Heaven. . . . The worshipper recedes three paces, and immediately the God is behind him, and in consequence he honors the God which is behind him. He advances five steps, and perceives [the God] before him, and in consequence he honors the God which is before him. Turning to the left he bends his body to honor the God, which is good, for the God is then on his left. Turning to the right he bends his body to honor the God, which is not so good, for the God is then on his right. He uplifts his head to honor the God, the God is above him; he lowers his head to honor the God, and the God is near him. Finally he worships the God, and it is honored in this act of worship.

Despite certain differences, this is unquestionably reminiscent of the genuflections of the Amidah, or "Standing Prayer," a central element in every Jewish service.

It is customary to take three steps back and then three steps forward prior to reciting the Amidah, and to do the same at its conclusion, when one also bows three times (to the left, right, and front). This gesture symbolizes the worshipper's approach toward and subsequent departure from God's throne. During the first and the second blessings, and the second from the last, it is customary to bend the knees and bow.[15]

B. D. Drenger, the editor of *The Haggadah of the Chinese Jews*, found some fascinating similarities between the 1489 inscription and the biblical account of Joseph and Pharaoh and of the Jewish migration to Egypt.

1. The 1489 inscription says: "Seventy families, viz., Li, Yen, Kao, Chao, and others, came to the Court of Song."

Exodus says: "And all the souls that came out of the loins of Jacob were seventy souls" (1:5).[16]

2. The 1489 inscription says: "bringing as tribute cloth of cotton from Western Lands."

Genesis says: ". . . take of the best products of the land in your vessel, and carry down to the man a present" (42:11).

3. The 1489 inscription says: "The emperor said, 'You have come to China. Keep and follow the custom of your forefathers, and settle at Kaifeng.' "

Genesis says: "The land of Egypt is before thee; in the best of the land let thy father and brothers dwell; let them dwell in the land of Goshen" (47:6).

Drenger concludes:

There are three salient facts which appear both on the Chinese tablets and in the Torah—the Figure 70, Tribute, and the Right to settle on the land. I believe it is rather a reenactment of the story of Jacob and Joseph in our Torah.[17]

The writings of Kaifeng Jewry share many ideas and concepts with other Jewish works as well. For instance (again the example comes from Drenger),[18] Ai Shi-de presented an inscription to the synagogue that says, "Its presence is not impeded by visible form, its absence does not imply an empty void; for the Way is outside the limits of existence or non-existence."[19] Compare what the great medieval philosopher Maimonides said in his Thirteen Principles of the Faith: "I believe with perfect faith that the Creator, blessed be his name, is not a body, and that he is free from all the accidents of matter, and that he has not any form whatsoever."[20]

To give one more example, let us look at a prayer in the Memorial Book:

May God remember the soul of my respected father, _____ son of _____, who has gone to his eternal home; on whose behalf I vow as alms _____; may his soul be bound up in Abraham, Isaac, and Jacob, Sarah, Rebekah, Rachel, and Leah, and all other righteous men and women that are in the Garden of Eden, and let us say, Amen.[21]

The similarity of this to the Yizkor prayer is striking. L. N. Dembitz points out that "in many Sephardic synagogues a 'Hashkabah' (laying to rest) for a long list of deceased members is read on Kol Nidre night; in others, vows for the dead are made in the daytime, between musaf and minchah." Leslie comments: "A comparison with the prayers found at the end of the registers, of men and women, is completely convincing."[22]

Another example is the Kaddish de-Rabbanan found at the front of the Memorial Book, described by Leslie as "close to the version of Maimonides and the Yemen."[23]

With the passage of time, variations developed in the external expression of the common faith. But it is easy to see the common core underlying the variations, consisting of weekly readings from the Torah and the Prophets, and of ancient formulations and rituals preserved unchanged from the original biblical ordinances or their elaborations in the Oral Law.

All this notwithstanding, the inscriptions of the Kaifeng Jews seem to have been strongly influenced by Confucianism, or as Leslie says, "the ideas expressed are sometimes Jewish in Confucian garb."

We must recall that these documents are written in Chinese, which makes a big difference in the way they are formulated. From a social-linguistic viewpoint, language is a form of social behavior associated with a specific social group that conditions its members' thinking in every sphere of life. Thus, as Edward Sapir, a well-known linguist, explains, "No two languages are ever sufficiently similar to be considered as representing the same social reality."[24]

It is not surprising, therefore, that the external expression of the inscriptions is "in Confucian garb" or under a strong Confucian influence. Since Judaism was a totally foreign matter to the Chinese, their language had no set phrases suitable for expressing Jewish ideas in the same way that English, French, and German, for example, all have more or less comparable theological terms for expressing ideas related to the common Judeo-Christian heritage of the West. The Kaifeng Jews had to borrow from the available Chinese expressions if they wanted to erect a stele in their synagogue courtyard with an inscription in Chinese that would tell about their faith to an audience that certainly included people who knew nothing about Judaism and Jewish terminology. The best example in point is the phrase "four times a month" used in the 1489 inscription to indicate the Sabbath. At that time the Chinese had no sense of the week as a division of time, and there was no term for "week" in their language, so it would have been meaningless to describe the Sabbath, in the usual way, as a weekly event.

None of the synagogue inscriptions includes even one reference that can be identified as a quotation from a book of the Hebrew Bible. Moreover, there are a number of references to the Chinese classics or actual quotations from them. To my mind, however, this was mainly done for the sake of convenience or as a matter of using the established Chinese literary idiom for such inscriptions.

Shi Jingxun, a Chinese historian from Kaifeng, says:

> . . . if they had not adorned it [their concept] with the words of the Confucians, those who listened to them would have covered their ears and left!
>
> . . . when Christian followers profess their scriptures, they are certain to cite the Four Books and the Five Classics [Confucian works] as a parallel; it is with this intention, this stele makes clear the purpose and main theme from the beginning.[25]

Andrew Plaks adds:

We must be careful not to over-interpret every point at which
loaded philosophical terms are inserted into these texts, since
such usages may often be taken as examples of the obligatory
decorative touches of formal prose style. This is clearly the
case in many references to "Heaven," the Dao, "the correct
teachings," and various specific Confucian virtues, as well as
the automatic condemnation of heretical thinking. It applies
just as well to the use of certain heterodox terms, such as the
notion of "sudden enlightenment" mentioned in the 1489
text. This does not necessarily indicate any measure of
Buddhist influence, since by this period such expressions
belong to a large common pool of philosophical vocabulary
shared by all of the schools of thought under the syncretic
umbrella of Neo-Confucianism.[26]

The issue is further clarified by an examination of the Kaifeng
writings in Hebrew, such as the prayers, the Memorial Book, and
the tablets on the walls of the synagogue. All of these were written
in the same period as the inscriptions. No Confucian teaching is
ever quoted in the Hebrew texts, and there is not even one expression from Chinese sources. What we see is frequent quotations
from the Hebrew Scriptures or other Jewish sources. The great contrast between the writings in Chinese and in Hebrew is proof that
statements were sometimes written in "Confucian garb" only for
the sake of convenience.

Confucianism began as a set of ethical teachings, and Judaism,
from its beginnings, has had a strongly ethical orientation. Five of
the Ten Commandments are purely ethical in content, and there
is an ethical aspect to the other five. That is why Judaism is sometimes described as ethical monotheism. Moreover, as has often
been noted, Judaism is not so much a religion as a way of life, and
this may have made it seem similar to Confucianism in the minds
of the Kaifeng Jews. I believe that it is in this sense that the 1663
inscription says: "The composition of the Scriptures, although
written in an ancient script [Hebrew] and of a different pronunci-

ation, is in harmony with the principles of the Six classics [of Confucianism], and in no case is there anything not in harmony with them."

An analysis of the Confucian material in the inscriptions shows that most of it, if not all, deals with ethical teachings and has nothing, or at least very little, to do with faith. For instance, the 1489 inscription says, "honoring the Way of Heaven venerating ancestors, giving high regard to the relations between the Prince and his ministers, being filial to parents, living in harmony with wife and children, preserving the distinction between superiors and inferiors, and having neighborly relations with friends." Clearly, these are moral teachings. Thus the real implication of the the 1489 inscription is that Confucianism and Judaism agree on essential points and differ only on secondary ones.

The religious life of Kaifeng Jewry was both strong and normative in the fifteenth to seventeenth centuries. The documents and materials offer valuable testimony to the strong Jewish identity of the community despite the apparently heavy influence of Confucianism. It is only in the sphere of morality that Confucian teachings are adopted or Chinese texts quoted. In short, Kaifeng Jewry in this period constituted a distinct, observant Jewish community. Despite long centuries of isolation, the Kaifeng Jews kept faith with what they remembered of Judaism, including observance of the Sabbath and other holidays, the practice of circumcision, and abstaining from non-kosher foods.

In *The Jews in China*, an anonymous missionary publication dating from 1843, the author says:

> Among their observances we find mention of Circumcision, Sabbath, Feast of Tabernacles, Rejoicing of the Law, and the Fast of Atonement. The Jesuit missionaries make no mention of Passover or Pentecost being kept at K'ai-feng Fu; but surely these could not have been neglected. Indeed, we shall see at a later day, that both were celebrated there till recently.[27]

Gozani, after his visit in 1704, noted the resistance to intermarriage: "These families marry one among another, and never with the Hui-hui, or Mohammedans, with whom they have nothing in common, either with regard to books, or religious ceremonies."[28] Although this is something of an exaggeration, it does tell us that the Kaifeng Jews regarded religion as a serious concern when marriage was contemplated. Since we know that many Kaifeng Jewish men had non-Jewish wives, it is possible that the community did not allow its daughters to contract marriages with anyone outside the religion, but permitted males to intermarry with Gentiles. The information in the Memorial Book shows that the Jin and Shi clans married out of the religion less often than the other clans.

The practice of the rite of circumcision by Kaifeng Jewry in the nineteenth century is attested by many accounts. For instance, the North China Herald reported in 1851, "The two Jews who have come to Shanghai . . . both received the rite of circumcision, which is still practiced on all male infants, within one month after birth."[29]

Ultimately, the Kaifeng Jews lost their ability to read Hebrew. The situation became worse when the last rabbi died. The synagogue was in ruins in the mid-nineteenth century and the community fell apart. However, the desire of Kaifeng Jews to learn the language never died.

In the early nineteenth century, the Kaifeng Jews "exposed their parchments in the market-place, in hope they might attract the attention of some wandering Jew who would be able to restore to them the language of their fathers."[30] Although they failed to find anyone who could help them, this effort illustrates their strong sense of identity and desire to revive the knowledge of Hebrew.

Not only did these Jews "appear to have a great desire to re-establish the Hebrew services in their synagogue, they have expressed also a willingness to send down their children for instruction. And they are now engaged in the study of Hebrew." [31]

MODERN TIMES

One of the strongest evidences of the continuing sense of Jewish identity of the Kaifeng Jews following the death of their last rabbi is the emotional letter they wrote in 1850 to Layton, the British consul in Fukien:

Morning and night, with tears in our eyes and with offering of incense, do we implore that our religion may again flourish. We have everywhere sought about, but could find none who understood the letters of the Great Country, and this has occasioned us deep sorrow. But now the unexpected arrival of your letter fills us with happiness. We heard that a letter had last year been received by one T'ieh, from a country of the West, but this to our regret we never got a sight of it. However, the receipt of your present letter assures us that the holy religion contains still a germ of vitality, and that in the great English nation the history of its origin has not been lost. If it shall be possible again to erect our temple, it will give joy not only to our own community, but likewise the holy men of T'ien-chu [God] will rejoice exceedingly. It will be needful, meanwhile, that the proceedings with a view to this end be conducted prudently and with caution.

Our synagogue in this place has long been without ministers; the four walls of its principal hall are greatly dilapidated, and the compartments of the hall of the holy men are in ruins. The ablution chamber and the repository [for the Scriptures] are in ruins likewise. Through the whole day have tears been in our eyes, and grief at our hearts, at the sight of such things. It has been our desire to repair the synagogue, and again to procure ministers to serve in it; but poverty prevented us, and our search was vain. Daily with tears have we called on the Holy Name. If we could again procure preacher ministers, and could put in order our synagogue, our religion would have a firm support for the future, and its sacred documents would have secure repository. This it needs no divination to be assured of.[32]

Despite their extreme poverty, the Kaifeng Jews sought nothing beyond assistance to restore knowledge of their religion. Their

desire to repair the synagogue and find rabbis to serve in it expresses their strong sense of identity.

> Day after day, year after year, they maintained themselves in
> the belief in the vitality of their faith, and the certainty that
> it would again flourish. They believe that no other desire
> could entertain them more. If nothing could help them, their
> last sole hope would be that after death their souls could
> return to God and be blessed.[33]

George Smith mentioned in 1851 in his *The Jews at K'ae-fung-
foo* that "some time previously, they had petitioned the Chinese
Emperor to have pity on their poverty, and to rebuild their temple.
No reply had been received from Peking, but to this feeble hope
they still clung."[34]

Jacob Liebermann reported in 1867 that the Kaifeng Jews were
willing to "offer a reward and leading position to anyone who
would be able to explain the wording of the Scroll."

There were several families who were strongly aware of their
Jewish ancestry in Kaifeng when Bishop Charles William White
arrived there to assume his Anglican ministry at the beginning of
the twentieth century.

The desire to rebuild the synagogue was reiterated by a Jewish
delegation from Kaifeng that visited Shanghai at the invitation of
the Society for the Rescue of the Chinese Jews, as was reported by
Walter Fuchs in the *T'ien Hsia Monthly*:

> Regarding the ancient temple site, they showed a more con-
> crete interest. The site was then a water-hole, and the origi-
> nal title deed had been lost for a long time. Lately, however,
> they had succeeded in securing a new deed issued by the
> Chinese authorities to them in the name of the seven clans.
> They wanted to affirm that in their coming to Shanghai they
> were not prompted by any hope of personal gain. . . . They
> wanted to be instructed in the religion of their forefathers,
> and if the synagogue could be rebuilt without too much delay,

"this," they said, "certainly would raise us from the dust and might rejuvenate the remnants of the ancient people."[35]

Again in 1932, when David A. Brown, a prominent American Jew, visited Kaifeng, he was told during a meeting with representatives of five of the seven Jewish clans that the most pressing need was a school for their children and that they were eager to return to Judaism if they could relearn it. Brown writes: "They know they are Jews, but know nothing of Judaism. They realize they are Chinese, completely assimilated, yet there is pride in the ancient people who are different from the other Chinese in Kaifeng."[36]

The Chinese Jews were still very much aware of their ancient heritage and eager to renew it.

W. A. P. Martin tells of his personal experiences in Kaifeng during his visit there in 1866:

"Are there among you any of the family of Israel?" I inquired. "I am one," responded a young man, whose face corroborated his assertion; and then another and another stepped forth, until I saw before me representatives of six out of the seven families into which the colony is divided.[37]

"I am one." What a clear and unhesitating voice! It poignantly expresses the continuing sense of identity of the Kaifeng Jews after the loss of their rabbi and the House of the Lord. This voice was not heard only once in history. It was echoed more than a hundred years later when Jin Xiaojing, who apparently belonged to the Jin clan of Kaifeng Jewry, published an article in a Chinese magazine with the title, "I Am a Chinese Jew."[38]

George Smith, in 1851, predicted that "after a few years all traces of Judaism will probably have disappeared and this Jewish remnant have been amalgamated with and absorbed into surrounding Mohammedanism."[39] More than a hundred years has elapsed since Smith made this prediction. What has happened to the descendants of Kaifeng Jewry?

TODAY

In 1985, Dr. Wendy Abraham decided to find out. Here is how she explained her reason for doing so:

> It has been shown that in the 1920's and 1930's many descendants had a clear understanding of their heritage and their place in Kaifeng's Jewish history. This knowledge could have conceivably been handed down to their children, who in 1985 were still able to remember these stories and offer this knowledge to their children.[40]

Abraham went to Kaifeng and interviewed a number of the city's Jewish descendants. She concluded that "they all displayed a strong awareness of their unique ethnic identity and a desire to instill this knowledge in their children."[41]

In 1997, a group of Jews visited Kaifeng. While there they held a Sabbath service that was attended by some of the descendants: "Quite spontaneously, Zhang's 14-year-old son, his father, and three members of the Shi family were called up to the Torah where they wore talits and repeated the prayers."[42]

Many reports confirm the impression that the surviving Kaifeng Jewish descendants still have a special feeling for their roots, as evidenced by their openness in confirming that they are descended from Jews, their desire to learn more about Jewish history and culture, and their willingness to contact Jews who live outside of China.

Abba Eban, the renowned Israeli diplomat and Jewish scholar, said of Spanish Jewry: ". . . although over the years they were influenced by the dress, the speech, and the customs of their Christian neighbors, at heart they remained fiercely loyal to their Jewishness and resistant to any change in their way of life."[43]

The essence of this comment is applicable to the situation of the Kaifeng Jews. As Dr. Beverly Friend has written:

> . . . the people we met in Kaifeng clearly were not impostors.

On our last night there, as we celebrated a Sabbath dinner with three descendants of Kaifeng Jews, we welcomed this link to our Asian family, so long lost and now—at last—able to learn about and participate in Jewish culture. For those of us who shared that Friday night meal, there was no doubt about how strongly these descendants feel their Jewish connection.[44]

Whether that feeling will eventually lead to the revival of this ancient community of Kaifeng, only history can tell.

[1] Donald D. Leslie, *The Survival of the Chinese Jews*, p. 102.

[2] Michael Pollak, *Mandarins, Jews, and Missionaries*, pp. 334–336.

[3] Benjamin J. Israel, *The Jews of India*, pp. 7–8.

[4] Ibid., p. 8.

[5] Xu Xin and Lin Jiyao, *Encyclopeadia Judaica*, p. 709.

[6] Kublin, *Studies of the Chinese Jews*, p. 210.

[7] The 1489 inscription. There is one additional character, Gu, which means "ancient," in front of this name.

[8] Chen Yuan: "A Study of the Israelite Religion in Kaifeng," p. 271.

[9] The 1663 inscription.

[10] Michael Pollak, *The Torah Scrolls of the Chinese Jews*, p. 114.

[11] The 1489 inscription.

[12] Ibid.

[13] The vertical tablet written by Ai Shih-te. See White, *Chinese Jews*, pt. II, p. 139.

[14] Pollak, *Mandarins, Jews, and Missionaries*, pp. 283–284.

[15] *Encyclopedia of Judaism*, p. 52.

[16] Some scholars argue that "seventy" in the inscription may be an error for "seventeen." It is neither a mistake nor an exact number, but, as Drenger says, "a reenactment of the story of Jacob and Joseph in the Torah." Cf. Chen Yuan's "A Study of the Israelite Religion in Kaifeng."

[17] B. D. Drenger, *The Haggadah of the Chinese Jews*, p. 11.

[18] Ibid., p. 12.

[19] White, *Chinese Jews*, pt. I, p. 126.

[20] See his commentary to Mishnah Sanhedrin.

[21] Cited by Leslie, *Chinese-Hebrew Memorial Book*, p. 158.

[22] Ibid., p. 20.

[23] Ibid., p. 162.

[24] David G. Mandelbaum, *Selected Writings of Edward Sapir*, p. 162.

[25] See his article in *Sino-Judaica*, vol. 1, p. 75.

[26] Andrew Plaks, "The Confucianization of the Chinese Jews," p. 31.

[27] White, *Chinese Jews*, pt. I, p. 75.

[28] Ibid., p.42.

[29] Ibid., p. 133.

[30] Ibid., p. 187.

[31] Ibid., p. 133.

[32] Ibid., pp. 86–87.

[33] Chao Nien-tzu's postscript to his letter to Finn. In White, *Chinese Jews*, pt. I, p. 88.

[34] Ibid., pt. I, p. 101.

[35] Ibid., p. 167.

[36] David A. Brown, "Brown Rediscovers China's Ancient Jews," p. 229.

[37] White, *Chinese Jews*, pt. I, p. 185.

[38] Jin Xiaojing, in *Universal Knowledge Quarterly* 4 (1981).

[39] White, *Chinese Jews*, pt. I, p. 102.

[40] Wendy Abraham, "Memories of Kaifeng's Jewish Descendants Today," p. 18.

[41] Ibid.

[42] Matthew Trustch and Jonathan Shulman, "Minyan in Kaifeng," p. 6.

[43] Abba Eban, *Heritage*, p. 212.

[44] Beverly Friend, "A Visit to Kaifeng," p. 37.

Chapter Five

Relations with Neighbors

Jews settled in Kaifeng by choice, not because they were forced to do so, and this was an important decision. Many tales arose among the Kaifeng Jews about the hospitable welcome their ancestors received from the Song court. These legends were repeatedly told orally by Gao Fu, Zhao Pingyu, Li Jinbiao, and other Kaifeng Jewish descendants. The one entitled "The Emperor Bestows Surnames" relates how the Jews were met by the Chinese emperor when they first came to Kaifeng.[1]

According to the legend, the emperor was very pleased with the newcomers and bestowed upon them his own surname and the names of his six ministers: Zhoa, Li, Ai, Zhang, Gao, Jin, and Shi.[2] He issued a decree stating: "You have come to our Central Plain [China]. Honor and preserve the customs of your ancestors, and remain and hand them down in Bianliang [Kaifeng]."[3]

Although the bestowal of surnames by the Song emperor remains purely anecdotal and unlikely, the decree has some credibility and is mentioned in the 1489 inscription. Historians and scholars, however, have failed to find any evidence or documents to prove that the meeting ever took place or that the decree was issued. Some scholars believe it is only a legend invented by the Jews in order to prove the legitimacy of their presence in Kaifeng.

The bestowal of a surname on an individual Jew by a Chinese emperor did happen, although much later, in 1423. According to the *Veritable Records of the Ming Emperor Dai Zhong*, An San, a Kaifeng Jew, was granted the surname Zhao by imperial decree and the rank of commissioner in the Embroidered Uniform Guard. He was called Zhao Cheng ever after.[4]

The positive feelings of the Kaifeng Jews about the Song dynasty derive from their decision to settle in its capital city. Additional proof lies in the fact that they continued to use the Song calendar after the dynasty was defeated by the Golden Tartars and fled from Kaifeng.

Chen Yuan comments:

> The 1489 inscription says the synagogue was built in the first year of the Long Xing period [1163] of Song Emperor Xiao Zong. This is the same as the third year of the Da Ding period of [Golden Tartar] Jin Emperor Shi Zong. By 1163 the Jin had been in occupation of Kaifeng for 38 years. Kaifeng people describing Kaifeng affairs of that time should have used the Jin dynasty calendar. The fact that the Jews did not, shows that they held orthodox concepts [regarding legitimacy of rule].[5]

Pan Guandan, the author of *Jews in Ancient China: A Historical Survey*, says further:

> Chen Yuan thinks this is because the Kaifeng Jews had "orthodox" concepts. There is something in that. But we believe it is because even by the Ming dynasty the Kaifeng Jews still were grateful to the Song Emperor who had accepted their tribute and welcomed them to "settle in Bianliang." This was before the [Song dynasty's] move to the south. And most likely funds for the building of the synagogue were also granted by the ruling Northern Song monarch. Later, though the ruling house was changed, the gratitude of the Jews continued for many years thereafter.[6]

Wu Zhelin, another Chinese scholar, makes the following remarks about the same event:

In referring to the erection of the first synagogue in 1163, the inscription states the time in terms of the Song dynastic period, although Kaifeng was then occupied by the Jin [Golden Tartars] and Song had moved its capital to Hangzhou. To thus stress the sovereignty of the Han Chinese several hundred years after the event demonstrates the friendly relations the Jews enjoyed with their hosts, and the gratitude they still felt for the freedom of religion which had been granted to them.[7]

RELATIONS WITH THE CHINESE AUTHORITIES

Relations between Jews and the governments of their host countries have often been critical. Jews worldwide always sought to maintain positive relations with the local authorities.

Mutual respect was the principal feature of the relations between Jews and the Chinese authorities.

The Jews showed great respect for the rulers of China from their initial arrival. One legend states that the Jewish newcomers brought white cotton cloth as entry tribute for the emperor (cotton was not grown in China at that time, and cotton cloth was rare and expensive).[8]

Generally, Chinese officials were ready to tolerate religious practices and other foreign beliefs, and to permit the existence of places of worship for beliefs and ceremonies of a purely religious nature so long as these did not conflict with Chinese concepts of empire or manifestly threaten the basis of Chinese sovereignty. On many known occasions, they were kind and generous to the Jews and treated them equally and without discrimination. The 1489 inscription of the synagogue testifies:

As soon as Emperor Kao Tai-tsu, of our great Ming dynasty, founded the dynasty, he first pacified the armies and people of the Empire. To all who responded to his beneficent influence, he bestowed land for settlement where they could live peacefully and happily follow their occupations. This was truly lack of favoritism and equal benevolence to all.

Relations between the Jews and the Chinese government were good, sometimes even excellent, because the Chinese officials respected Jewish traditions and customs. For instance, the government once enacted a regulation that "strangers and carriers of pork cannot pass near the synagogue."[9]

The good relations between the Kaifeng Jews and the government are further shown by the grants of land by officials of different dynasties for the building or rebuilding of the synagogue

There is a presumption that in 1163 special permission was requested and granted to construct a unique building for the synagogue in Kaifeng. Presumably the same kind of permission was requested and granted each time the synagogue was destroyed, either by fire or by flood. The reconstruction in 1421 was under the direct sponsorship of the prince of Zhou, who was the younger brother of Ming emperor Chen Zu. The project was subsidized by the Imperial Cash Office.[10] In 1461, a flood destroyed the synagogue completely except for its foundation. After the floodwaters subsided, the Jews of Kaifeng, headed by Ai Qin, petitioned the provincial commissioner, requesting a decree confirming the right of the community to rebuild the demolished synagogue on the original site of the ancient one. The permission was soon granted, and Kaifeng Jewry was able to reconstruct the house of worship; it was dedicated in 1489.[11]

Similar situations occurred in 1279, 1512, and 1663. To express their gratitude to the authorities and to signify imperial approval, the Kaifeng Jews placed a special tablet in the synagogue acknowledging their allegiance to the emperor.[12] According to Ch'iu T'ien-sheng, a Chinese Christian who visited the Kaifeng synagogue in December 1850, the imperial tablet for the Ming dynasty read: "May the Great Ming Dynasty rule a myriad years."[13]

Ever after, it became a tradition for the Jewish community of Kaifeng to maintain such a tablet in the synagogue. It was displayed in the same place in the synagogue after the Qing court replaced the Ming in 1644, although the wording was changed: "May the Emperor of the Great Qing Dynasty rule for ten thousand years, ten thousand years, and ten thousand myriad years."[14] This practice is strikingly similar to the prayer for the sovereign recited in synagogues in the United Kingdom.

The close relations between the Jews and the authorities can also be seen from the celebration in 1663 honoring the dedication of the newly completed synagogue that replaced the one destroyed in the Yellow River flood of 1642. To honor the Jewish community, Chinese officials of different ranks and from various places in China presented gifts called *pien* that are traditionally given in honor of the dedication of a building. *Pien* (literally "horizontal tablets") are painted or lacquered boards, three feet in length and about two feet wide, bearing an inscription that embodies a moral precept. A traditional gift of this kind reflected the respect of the giver for the recipient.

There were thirteen signed *pien* in the synagogue. Twelve of them were written and presented by Chinese officials. Let us take a closer look at the texts of the *pien* and the names and titles of the Chinese officials who presented them to the Jewish community:

Hu Shi-mei, Imperial Envoy to Honan for the Xingdun Circuit and Junior Adviser, dedicated "Religion Is Derived from Heaven."

Wang Yuan-fu, Assistant Defense Commandant of the Daliang Circuit of Honan and Senior Counselor, composed "Religion Follows the Truth of Heaven."

Li Guang-zo, Assistant Provincial Treasurer of Fujian and Intendant of the Xingquan Circuit and Junior Counselor, prepared "Invisible Source of the Law."

Xi Shi, Prefect of Kaifeng Fu, indicted "Honor Heaven and Pray for the Country."

Shen Xu, District Magistrate of Kaifeng and of Qiang-Jiang, composed "Hall of the Bright Mirror."

Qian Xiang-qian, District Magistrate of Xiang-fu County and of Chuyang, presented "With Enlightenment Serve the Supreme Ruler."

Xu, Imperial Envoy for the control of the Yellow River Circuit and the Waterways of Honan and Assistant Provincial Judge with additional step of merit, composed "He Whom the Religion Honours Has No Form."

Xu Hua-cheng, Governor of Chu and of Peking, erected "Lord of the Religion of Purity."

Xu Hua-cheng, Provincial Treasurer of Peking, composed "Render Pure Service to Majestic Heaven."[15]

Most significantly, two of the *pien*, dated 1658, were presented to the synagogue by imperial decree. The texts read: "He Daily Regards This Place" and "August Heaven the Supreme Ruler."[16] The imperial decree certainly amplified the message conveyed by the legends.

As Leslie observes: "There can be very few cities in the world which can boast of a continuous Jewish community and synagogue extending well over 700 years. This implies a measure of toleration, but may also be the consequence of the Chinese governmental system of treating minorities as such."[17]

Obviously, the Jewish community of Kaifeng earned the respect and friendship of Chinese officialdom, in striking contrast with the experiences of their brethren in Christian or Islamic society during the same period. It is worth pointing out that this had much to do with Jewish achievement. One cannot imagine such good relations having existed had the Jews not achieved so much.

RELATIONS WITH THE POPULACE

The Jews of Kaifeng also appear to have established good relations with the Chinese people among whom they lived and worked.

Genuine friendship is attested by the many intermarriages. As shown by the information in the Memorial Book, about fifty different Chinese clans allowed their daughters to marry Kaifeng Jews. This kind of family tie through marriage would not have come about unless there had been close relations between Jews and non-Jews, because no Chinese family in that period would have given its daughters to strangers or enemies.

The excellent relations between Jews and Chinese over an extended period are illustrated by solid evidence derived from the inscriptions on the synagogue stelae. Each and every stele shows that some Chinese were so friendly to the community that they were willing to have their names included in the inscription. Each time a stele was made, there were always Chinese among the donors who paid for it. Cao Zho, a Chinese graduate of the *Lin-shan* grade who was skilled in writing Chinese script, penned the characters for the 1489 stele. Fu Ju, another *Lin-shan* graduate, wrote the seal characters in an ancient seal character style at the top of the stele because of his skill in calligraphy.

When the 1512 stele was prepared, other Chinese were involved and contributed to it. The text of the stele was composed by Zho Tang, a senior official. Kao Fang, the recipient of a doctoral degree (*Jin Shi*), wrote the inscription in vermilion for the engraver. Xu Ang, another *Jin Shi*, wrote the seal characters at the top of the inscription. These three Chinese were senior officials and occupied very prestigious posts. Zho Tang obtained his *Jin Shi* title in 1496 and served both as state counselor of Guangdong Province and adviser to the governor of Sichuan Province. According to the list of Ming dignitaries of the second class of the fourth grade, Kao Fang was a secretary of the Supervising Censors and had formerly been a writer in the Hanlin Academy. Xu Ang was also a secretary of the Supervising Censors.

The Chinese who were involved in preparing the 1663 stele were either imperial ministers or imperial envoys. Liu Cang, an imperial minister, second classical tutor of the emperor, and first tutor of the crown prince, composed the text. Li Guang-zuo, an imperial envoy, provincial commander-in-chief, assistant provincial judge in Yunnan, and literary chancellor, wrote the characters in vermilion for the engravers. Hou Liang-han, an imperial envoy, provincial commander-in-chief, and literary chancellor, wrote the seal characters at the top.

A few more words are in order about Liu Cang, who composed the text of the 1663 stele. He was a great scholar and an imperial minister of the Chinese court. He served as second classical tutor of the emperor and first tutor of the crown prince. He was also president of the Board of Punishments and president on leave of the Board of Public Works. He obtained his doctorate in 1625 and died in 1670. As a native of Kaifeng, he developed friendships with the leading members of the Jewish community, such as Zhao Ying-cheng, a major of the royal army. And through these contacts he was quite familiar with the life and faith of Kaifeng Jewry.

There is no doubt that he was a trusted and intimate friend of Kaifeng Jewry. In his own words,

I am a native of Pien [Kaifeng], and have known the religion of Israel for some time, and moreover have been on terms of intimate friendship with Major Chao Ch'eng-chi, the Assistant Grand Treasurer Chao ying-ch'eng, and the official physician Ai Hsien-sheng, so that from the beginning to the end I am quite able to relate these matters in details.[18]

Because of this, Liu was invited by Major Zhao to compose the 1663 inscription when the community received permission to rebuild the synagogue. He spared no effort in studying "the old records" and, as he wrote in the inscription, took great care so that "men might know the origin and history of the Law of Moses . . . and recognize that the merit of all the members of the religion is such as cannot be obliterated."[19]

Shen Quan was another friend of the Kaifeng Jews. He wrote three couplets—vertical presentation tablets on which antithetical honorific couplets were written in vertical columns that would be hung in pairs on adjacent pillars or on the doorjambs of the

entrance of a building—and presented them as gifts to the synagogue. His couplets read:

> From the time of Noah, when beauteous creation arose, until
> now, talented men of the West Region have sought the
> principle that produced Heaven, Earth, and Man;
> From the time of Abraham, when our religion was estab-
> lished, and subsequently, men of China have diffused
> instruction, and obtained complete knowledge of
> Confucianism, of Buddhism, and of Taoism.

> Before the Great Void, we burn the fragrant incense, entirely
> forgetting its name or form;
> Tracing back to the Western World, we resist our evil desires,
> and solely attend to purity and truth.

> The First Ancestor [Abraham] alone received the religion
> from Heaven and honoured Heaven, therefore we remem-
> ber the Ancestor;
> When living he was able to prevent and abstain from killing
> [Isaac], therefore we preserve life.[20]

From these verses, it is evident that Shen's knowledge of
Judaism transcended the average. He had many and deep contacts
with Kaifeng Jews and had often discussed their religion and way
of life. The couplets show that he tried to understand Judaism,
though from a Confucian perspective. As a non-Jew, his treatment
of Judaism is certainly something extraordinary when compared
with parallels in Western or Muslim countries prior to modern
times.

Shen's three couplets were displayed on the two principal pillars
immediately inside the eastern door of the Front Hall, the first pair
of large pillars in the inner part of the synagogue (i.e., where the
Ark of the Sacred Scriptures was set up, in the Rear Hall) and the
two pillars nearest to the "Bethel," or Ark of the Sacred
Scriptures.[21]

As part of their effort to maintain good relations with their neighbors, the Jews of Kaifeng diligently tried to understand Chinese culture—Confucianism—and seek a common ground. After years of study and observation of Confucianism, their findings were as follows:

> . . . in their main focus of ideas and established practices both [Judaism and Confucianism] are exclusively concerned with honoring the Way of Heaven, venerating ancestors, valuing the relations of ruler and subject, obedience to parents, harmony within families, correct ordering of social hierarchies, and good fellowship among friends: nothing more than the "five cardinal relations" of mankind.
>
> Although it [Judaism] differs from Confucian texts in its writing system, if one scrutinizes its basic principles he will find that it is the same, as it contains the Way of constant practices.[22]

Whether these quotations from the stelae are "not much more than self-serving propaganda" or "designed to find favor in the eyes of Chinese neighbors and Confucian authorities with some loyalty to the throne,"[23] they certainly show that the Kaifeng Jews tried to lay a common base with the Chinese for friendship and mutual understanding. It obviously worked, because there were never any conflicts between the two cultures.

The Kaifeng Jews did what they could to be good citizens of the city in which they lived. After the 1642 flood, they went to great lengths to help their Chinese neighbors even though they themselves faced the great challenge of rebuilding their temple and homes. In 1652, headed by Zhao Shi-fang, Kaifeng's Jews helped to rebuild a Chinese Confucian shrine in their neighborhood,[24] a gesture that surely won many friends.

CHINESE KNOWLEDGE AND ATTITUDES

Very few ordinary Chinese, especially those who had no contacts with Jews, would have had much understanding of the Jewish way of life and faith. Thus the Chinese people as a whole saw little if any difference between Jews and the other foreign peoples that had come to China from the west.

However, the residents of Kaifeng were somewhat more familiar with Jews and Judaism than most other Chinese. From living side by side over the centuries, they were aware that the Jews had different traditions and customs. The various names for the city's Jews provide an idea of what the local people knew about them and their religious heritage.

For instance, from the name *Gu Jiao* ("ancient religion"), one can infer that the local Chinese acknowledged the great antiquity of the Jews and their religion.

For a long time, Kaifeng's Jews were also called *Tiao-Jing-Jiao* ("The Sect That Plucks Out the Sinews"), a name reflecting the practice, ultimately based on Genesis 32:33, of removing the sciatic nerve from the hindquarters of animals slaughtered for food. This would seem to indicate some awareness of the dietary laws— at the very least that Jews refrained from eating certain foods.

Another name was *Lan Mao Hui Hui* ("People Who Wear Blue Hats"). Quite obviously, the local Chinese knew that Jews covered their heads at religious services and perhaps all of the time; moreover, they knew there was a difference between Jews and Muslims, who similarly covered their heads but wore white hats.

Finally, the Kaifeng Jews were referred to as *Jiao-Jing-Jiao* ("The Sect That Teaches the Scriptures"), a name indicating that their neighbors knew they possessed, treasured, and studied an extensive body of sacred literature that played a role in Judaism not unlike that of the Confucian classics in Chinese life. This understanding of the importance of the scriptures in Jewish life is further shown by the fact that the street adjoining the original site of the Kaifeng synagogue and passing through what was once the city's Jewish district is still called "Teaching the Torah Lane" even today.

The Chinese also knew that Jews used Hebrew in their prayers and had Torah scrolls written on parchment. In 1859, Hung Jen-kan, younger brother of the leader of the Taiping Uprising, wrote, "There are in the Hsiangfu district, K'aifeng County, Honan province, many Jews who wrote Hebrew characters on parchment."[25]

Overall, the Jews of Kaifeng seem to have felt safe and secure as a minority in Chinese society. Perhaps the only time they experienced fear was in the second half of the nineteenth century, when hostility to Christians (especially missionaries), Muslims, and foreigners in general was widespread and intense, a development reflecting China's lack of power and its continuing humiliation by other countries. As Leslie says,

> All the reports and contacts of foreigners are tinged with this feeling of fear, and suspicion. One of the few descriptions of the Kaifeng Jews by a Chinese is given by Havret from c. 1861. This is a fantastic and ignorant mixture of scraps from the Kaifeng Jewish inscriptions and the Sian Nestorian monument. The Jews (and Nestorians) are tarred with the anti-missionary brush.[26]

RELATIONS WITH MUSLIMS

The Chinese cities where Jews lived all had sizable Muslim communities. Kaifeng was no exception; it has long had a large and flourishing Muslim community. Even during the Golden Age of Kaifeng Jewry the city's Muslim population far outnumbered the Jews. Since the place of origin of the Kaifeng Jews was doubtless a Muslim country, probably Persia, they were certainly familiar with the faith and customs of the Chinese Muslims from the very outset.

The Jews and Muslims of Kaifeng lived side by side. Many of them were neighbors and friends. Of course, each group kept to its own traditions and tried to prevent the Chinese from confusing it with the other. This was necessary because the Chinese tended to be most aware of the similarities between Islam and Judaism, not surprisingly since these were the areas in which the two differed most radically from Chinese tradition and practice. Islam and Judaism both came from a region west of China. Both believed in one God and avoided idols and images. Both abstained from pork and had special slaughtering laws. Both practiced circumcision.

The similarity of Judaism and Islam in Chinese eyes is reflected in the fact that very often the same Chinese words are used to designate aspects of the two religions in the surviving documents of the Jewish and Muslim communities. The Chinese terms for Jewish and Muslim houses of worship and for Jewish and Muslim communal leaders are the same, but it is uncertain which sect used these terms first. According to Zhao Xiangrou, a Kaifeng Jewish descendant, it was the Jews.

> The Kaifeng Jews widely used the term *Qing-zhen* to describe their religion. The meaning of the term is actually defined clearly in the 1489 inscription. . . . The definition certainly gives new meaning to the combination of those two Chinese characters, which never existed before. However, the term was adopted by Chinese Muslims to describe their religion and their mosques. Today, most people do not know this development and mistakenly thought that the term was originally created by Muslims. For instance, many Chinese reference books define the phrase *Qing-zhen* as "a Muslim term." However, history proves that it is Jews who first used it to describe the religion. According to the *Handbook of Nationalities*, it was used to describe the religion of Islam in the Ming dynasty's Hong Zhi period [1488–1521]. Ma Shouqian, a Chinese scholar who wrote the chapter on the Hui nationality [Chinese Muslims], traces the development of Islam in China and says: "The religion of Islam in China follows the development of the Hui nationality and changed as it developed. It changed from the Ming through the early Qing; an important indication is that the religion of Islam integrated its tradition with those of China. Originally their houses of worship had names such as *Qing-jing* (pure and quiet), *Qing-xiu* (pure study), *Jing-jue* (pure feelings), *Zhen-jiao* (true teaching). The mosques gradually came to be called *Qing-Zhen Si* (Temple of Purity and Truth). At the same time, the religion of Islam in China began to be called the *Qing-Zhen Jiao* (Religion of Pure Truth). However, the Kaifeng

Jews began to use it as early as 1163 when they built their synagogue in Kaifeng. Therefore, the Jews were the first to use
the term to represent the religion and religious activities.[27]

As a small minority, the Kaifeng Jews wanted to keep their identity distinct so as not to be swallowed up by the much larger
Muslim population. They changed the name of the synagogue in
order to prevent confusion. Chen Yuen observes:

> In Yuan times (13th century) the synagogue was called Gu
> Cha Qing Zhen Si (Ancient Temple Synagogue of Purity and
> Truth). In the early Ming (14th century) the same name was
> used in an application to rebuild. This is stated in the 1489
> inscription.
>   But the 1512 inscription avoids the term "Purity and
> Truth" and speaks only of the "Ancient Temple." The aim
> was obvious. At that time the Muslims called their mosques
> Qing Zhen Si (Temple of Purity and Truth). Zuo Tang, the
> composer, deliberately chose the term Zun Chong Dao Jing Si
> (Synagogue Which Respects the Scriptures of the Way) to
> prevent any confusion.[28]

Another example is that the Kaifeng Jews willingly accepted the
name Tiao-Jin-Jiao ("Sect That Plucks Out the Sinews") because it
too differentiated them from the Muslims.

The reports on Jewish-Muslim relations by visitors to Kaifeng
are both complicated and contradictory. For instance, Ricci says,
"These Jews feel unfriendly towards that sect [the Muslims] and
abhor it."[29] Leslie comments: "Though no love was lost between
the Jews and Muslims, non-Chinese customs common to both
meant that many of those Jews who finally assimilated were swallowed up by Islam."[30]

Some believe that there was a tendency toward intermarriage
between the two groups, others that they tried hard to avoid such
links. Gozani wrote in 1704: "These [Jewish] families marry one
among another, and never with the hui-hui, or Mohammedans,

with whom they have nothing in common, either with regard to books, or religious ceremonies. They even turn up their whiskers in a different manner."[31]

Sergeant T'ieh, a Muslim from Kaifeng, says: "Six families have intermarried with the Chinese. Two families intermarry with the Mohammedans only. The Jews give their daughters to the Mohammedans; the Mohammedans do not give their daughters to the Jews."[32]

In 1851, Smith reported, "The Jews at K'ai-feng Fu are not allowed to intermarry with heathens and Mohammedans."[33]

In modern times, the Kaifeng Jews are sometimes mistaken for a Muslim sect and are referred to as "Blue Hat Muslims." This deadly mistake, which appears very often in articles and books, especially in interpretations of *Lan Mao Hui Hui*, a Chinese designation for Jews, reflects the Chinese use of the term *hui hui*. For many hundreds of years, Jews and Muslims in Kaifeng, as well as certain other ethnic groups from outside of China, were all called *hui hui*, a term that eventually became part of their more specific designations in Chinese. The Chinese term *hui hui* is misleading nowadays because in modern times its meaning has narrowed and only means people who are of the Muslim faith, but it had a much broader connotation in the past.

As explained in Chapter 1, foreign traders and merchants began coming to China with the opening up of the Silk Road in ancient times. Whether they were from countries in western Asia, the Middle East, or Europe, in Chinese eyes all foreigners were regarded as coming from the West. Finding it difficult to differentiate the newcomers on the basis of nationality or religion, the Chinese applied the general term *hui hui* to all of them, which at that time meant "people who come from the west."

Later, as foreigners began to settle in China, the native Chinese began to be able to tell one group from another on the basis of its faith or customs. For instance, in Kaifeng, Chinese used the term "White Hat *Hui Hui*" for Muslims, and *Shi Zi Hui Hui* ("Westerners of the Cross") for Christians because they often wore a cross to symbolize their faith. Jews were "Blue Hat *Hui Hui*" because the

Jewish men customarily wore blue hats. The evolution of *hui-hui* was noted by Ricci, who says:

> The Chinese call all these foreigners *hui-hui*, from which name we cannot learn their origin. The Mohammedans they call the *hui-hui* of the three laws (*san-chiao*); the Jews they call the *hui-hui* who extract the sinews from the meat which they eat; the Christians they call the *hui-hui* of the word for ten (i.e., cross).[35]

Nowadays *hui hui* refers chiefly to Muslims. Because both Jews and Muslims were called *hui hui* in the past, scholars unfamiliar with the term's origin mistakenly interpret "Blue Hat *Hui Hui*" as "Blue Hat Muslims," which is totally wrong. The Kaifeng Jews apparently disliked this designation, however, according to Gozanus. [35]

RELATIONS WITH OTHER MINORITIES

The Jews in Kaifeng also interacted with Tartars, Mongols, and other ethnic groups in Chinese society. They lived under the rule of the Tartars and the Mongols for about a hundred years each, and their relations with these peoples were generally good.

The Jews received permission to build their first synagogue in Kaifeng in 1163 from the Tartars. The synagogue was rebuilt during the reign of the Yuan emperor Kublai Khan in 1279. Obviously, it was the Mongols who granted permission for the rebuilding. While we have little information about how the Kaifeng Jews were treated by the Mongols, relations are believed to have been friendly. Jews in the Mongol Empire were "allowed to worship their own God, to engage in commerce and trade, and to become officials and soldiers."[36] They were also hired to serve as financial advisers and tax collectors and enjoyed some privileges.[37] Nonetheless, the Mongols imposed restrictions and prohibitions on certain Jewish customs and traditions, such as circumcision, ritual slaughter, and marriage between paternal cousins.[38]

RELATIONS WITH THE JESUITS AND CHRISTIANITY

The history of Kaifeng Jewry would be incomplete without some discussion of their relations with Christian missionaries, initially Jesuits and later Protestants of various denominations. The very fact that anything is known about Kaifeng Jewry in the West has much to do with its contacts with foreign missionaries, beginning with the meeting between Ai Tien and Father Matteo Ricci in Peking in 1605.

For the Jesuits, the discovery of the Kaifeng community had two important dimensions: the possibility of obtaining an authentic text of the Bible and the opportunity to broaden the scope of their missionary activities in China.[39]

Many Christian theologians had long believed that the Hebrew Bible, or Old Testament, as it had come down to them over the centuries, was neither complete nor reliable. Christian polemicists had insisted for well over a millennium that the text of the Hebrew Bible had been tampered with. To begin with, the New Testament contained several passages which purported to be quotations from the Old Testament but could not be found there. Since they were unwilling to doubt the reliability of the New Testament, they could only conclude that the Old Testament text available to them was incomplete. Moreover, it seemed inconceivable that the Jewish Scriptures could have failed to foretell the coming of the Christ in very specific terms. The absence of any prophecies relating to this epochal event from the Hebrew Bible made it self-evident that all such passages must have been excised or rewritten.

As Christians saw it, the rabbis of the talmudic era, in the centuries immediately following the time of Jesus, had expunged or altered the biblical verses predicting Christ's birth and ministry. Surmising that the version of the Torah possessed by the Kaifeng community might be so old as to predate the life of Jesus and thus not to have gone through this process, they hoped that by comparing a Torah scroll from Kaifeng with the standard Hebrew text of the Old Testament, they would be able to demonstrate that the

Hebrew Bible was "corrupt." With this end in mind, they tried to get access to the Torah scrolls in the Kaifeng synagogue.

The Jesuits had gone to China to preach Christianity and convert as many Chinese as possible. After many year's work, they had succeeded in converting quite a few Chinese, but they had begun to realize that they had undertaken an extremely difficult task. When compared with the total population of China, their converts made up a very small number. One of the major obstacles was that the Chinese lacked certain fundamental convictions that made people in the West receptive to theistic religion. Buddhism, Taoism, and Confucianism were not God-oriented; they did not extol the holiness of a deity or set forth a series of specific acts and moral demands that were said to be of divine origin and therefore incumbent on worshipers.

Chinese philosophers were concerned with enabling the individual to become more in harmony with the essence of life. In Christian eyes, however, the Chinese seemed to be polytheistic and idolatrous. It was very difficult to make them accept Christ. The Jesuits reasoned that the Jews might be another matter. Thus as soon as they learned of their presence in China, the Jesuits began contemplating the conversion of the Kaifeng Jews. They believed that it would be much easier to convert them because they shared the same creation stories and belief in an omnipotent God, the same Bible (at least the Old Testament), and the same prophets. While earlier experiences in Europe told them that the Jews were a strong-minded people, unwilling to give up their faith, the Jews of Kaifeng, they reasoned, might be different. Kaifeng's Jews had been isolated in this far-off land for centuries and seemed to be on the verge of extinction as a religious entity.

Father Ricci himself believed that the conversion of the Kaifeng Jews would not be difficult. "It appears to me that the Chinese Jews could . . . be easily led to the recognition of the true Messiah and into conversion to Christianity."[40]

Ricci asked the Jesuit general in Rome to assign one or two fathers versed in the Hebrew language to the task of winning over the Kaifeng Jews. Meanwhile, he sent a member of his mission to

Kaifeng with a letter to the rabbi explaining the origin and meaning of Christianity.[41] The mission was a failure, but the Jesuits would not give in. Over the next few years, they continued to send priests to visit the community, and finally in 1628, they established a church within walking distance of the Kaifeng synagogue. They continued to visit the synagogue and contact individual Jews. The Kaifeng Jews were displeased by the constant attempts to convert them and soon became very cautious. Visitors who came to the community to discuss the Torah or carry on a dialogue in Hebrew were welcome, but those who wanted to talk about the New Testament and Jesus were not. Such visitors were not even permitted to glimpse their copy of the Pentateuch. Thus, for instance, "The rabbi . . . even refused to draw back the curtains surrounding the synagogue Torah scroll [for Fr. Giulio Aleni], thus denying him as much as a glimpse of the Pentateuch."[42] Later on, missionaries reported:

> So long as they thought that the Father was of their faith, they gave him a magnificent welcome and listened with great joy to the stories of the Old Testament patriarchs; but once they noticed the pictures in his Bible, abominable in their eyes, they understood he was a Christian of the Cross who worshipped Jesus, whom they called Isai, a name taken from the Moors [Muslims], and they immediately charged about, urging the Father to leave the synagogue, which they thought had been profaned by his presence. He would have liked to discuss the Bible with them, but it was of no use. They had suddenly grown distrustful, and conversation no longer suited them.[43]

Initially, the Kaifeng Jews were pleased to meet Jesuit visitors. Contacts with outsiders were welcome because they provided opportunities to better their Hebrew knowledge or reestablish ties with co-religionists. The fact that the Jews invited the Jesuit Ricci to serve as their grand rabbi testifies to their need. Ricci realized that the Kaifeng Jews were more friendly to him than the remnants of Christianity left in China from an earlier era, none of whom were Catholics.[44] Leslie observes that "It must have been a great shock to the Jews to see Gozani driven out in disgrace in the anti-missionary persecution of 1724."[45]

From the mid-nineteenth century on, Kaifeng Jewry was frequently visited by Protestants. In 1850, for instance, two Chinese Protestants were sent from Shanghai to visit them. The following year two Jews from Kaifeng accompanied them back to Shanghai and reportedly studied Hebrew under one of the missionaries there.[46] In 1866, Rev. W. A. P. Martin visited the community. The Kaifeng Jews were delighted to receive messages from Jews elsewhere via Christian visitors and trusted them to deliver their own letters to Jewish communities abroad. The continuing missionary activity brought both anxiety and excitement. Renewed contacts with Christians awakened hopes of finding or reestablishing ties with Jews outside of China. If this was accomplished, the Jews of Kaifeng might be able to reestablish their religion, which had been on a downward trend since the 1850 destruction of the synagogue.

The most important and meaningful contacts between Protestants and Kaifeng Jewry were established by Bishop William Charles White in the early twentieth century. White was the head of the Canadian Anglican Mission in Kaifeng, which began its activities in 1910. Over the next twenty-five years, he had constant direct contact with the Kaifeng Jews. His book *Chinese Jews*, published in 1942, provides a wealth of background information about the life and situation of the Kaifeng Jewish community and is a handy source for studying it.

Thanks to the visits and effort of these Jesuits and Protestants, our knowledge and understanding of Kaifeng Jewry is much richer. Their reports and writings are important sources for modern-day scholars who want to study the history and life of the Kaifeng Jews.

[1] Wang Yisha, *Spring and Autumn of the Chinese Jews*, p. 149.
[2] Ibid.
[3] Ibid. The 1489 inscription bears the same text.
[4] *Veritable Records of the Ming Emperor Dai Zhong*, vols. 230–237.

[5] Chen Yuan, "A Study of the Israelite Religion in Kaifeng." In Sidney Shapiro, *Jews in Old China*, p. 24.

[6] Pan Guandan, *Jews in Ancient China*. In Shapiro, *Jews in Old China*, p. 55.

[7] Wu Zhelin, preface to Pan, *Jews in Ancient China*, p. 9.

[8] Wang, *Spring and Autumn of the Chinese Jews*, p. 3.

[9] William C. White, *Chinese Jews*, pt. I, p. 80.

[10] Pan, *Jews in Ancient China*. In Shapiro, *Jews in Old China*, p. 238.

[11] The 1489 inscription.

[12] The 1489 inscription mentions the tablet.

[13] White, *Chinese Jews*, p. 128.

[14] Ibid.

[15] Ibid., pt. II, pp. 125–134.

[16] Ibid., pp. 123–124.

[17] Donald D. Leslie, *The Survival of the Chinese Jews*, p. 112.

[18] The 1663 inscription.

[19] Ibid.

[20] White, *Chinese Jews*, pt. II, pp. 138, 140, and 142.

[21] Ibid.

[22] The 1663 inscription.

[23] Plaks, "Confucianization of the Chinese Jews," p. 30.

[24] Leslie, *Survival of the Chinese Jews*, p. 43.

[25] Ibid., p. 72.

[26] Ibid., pp. 60–61.

[27] See Zhao Xiangruo's paper delivered at the international conference on "Jews in China."

[28] In Shapiro, *Jews in Old China*, p. 25.

[29] Gallagher, *China in the Sixteenth Century*, Appendix II, p. 210.

[30] Leslie, "Kaifeng Jewish Community"; Kublin, *Studies of the Chinese Jews*, p. 192.

[31] Leslie, *Survival of the Chinese Jews*, p. 112.

[32] Ibid., p. 113.

[33] White, *Chinese Jews*, pt. I, p. 112.

[34] Leslie, *Survival of the Chinese Jews*, p. 35.

[35] Gozanus says that "to distinguish themselves from the Moors (with whom they share the common name Hui-hui), they call themselves and

are called T'iao-chin-chaio." Dehergne and Leslie, *Juifs de Chine*, p. 60.

[36] Leslie, *Survival of the Chinese Jews*, p. 111.

[37] Rossabi, "Muslim and Central Asian Revolts in Late Ming and Early Ch'ing."

[38] See the *Official History of the Yuan* and *Statutes of the Yuan*.

[39] Gallagher, *China in the Sixteenth Century*, Appendix II; Kublin, *Studies of the Chinese Jews*, p. 212.

[40] Leslie, *Survival of the Chinese Jews*, p. 115.

[41] Cf. Gallagher, *China in the Sixteenth Century*.

[42] Pollak, *Mandarins, Jews, and Missionaries*, p. 17.

[43] Unpublished translation by Dehergne and Leslie, from a manuscript held in Rome of de Geuvea's *Asia Extrema*, composed in 1644. Cf. Pollak, *Mandarins, Jews, and Missionaries*, p. 18.

[44] Leslie, *Survival of the Chinese Jews*, p. 115.

[45] Ibid.

[46] White, *Chinese Jews*, pt. I, p. 133.

Chapter Six

Jews in Other Chinese Cities

Kaifeng was not the only place where Jews resided in China. In fact, Jews were living in several other Chinese cities far earlier than in Kaifeng.

However, in many respects we know even less about the Jews in other cities than about the Kaifeng Jews. The beginnings of the Jewish Diaspora in China are buried in the dim past and are as obscure as the beginnings of the Jewish people. There few reliable documents, but many theories and speculations. The dates for the beginning of Jewish settlement in China range from biblical times to the Tang dynasty in the seventh to tenth centuries.

THE BIBLICAL PERIOD

The theories that place Jewish migrations to China in the biblical period are no more than legends or wild guesses based on vague or misunderstood scriptural references. Some believe that Jews first came to China after the destruction of the First Temple (586 B.C.E.) or even during the reign of Solomon (10th cent. B.C.E.). Some scholars accept a host of speculations related to the where-abouts of the Ten Lost Tribes or deduce a conclusion from the fol-lowing passage (Isaiah 49:12):

Behold, these shall come from far;
And, lo, these from the north and from the west,
And these from the land of Sinim.[1]

Based on this passage and other presumed evidence, Hieromonach Alexei Vinogradoff, a nineteenth-century Russian churchman, argued that there was trade between the Middle East and China in the time of David and Solomon. Its main agents, he claimed, were the Phoenicians, with the aid of the Israelite navy in the Red Sea built by Solomon.[2]

Nowadays, scholars reject Vinogradoff's notion because his assumptions are scarcely convincing and lack any supporting evidence. The word Sinim, in fact, does not mean "China," but refers to Syene in Upper Egypt.[3]

THE TALMUDIC ERA

The theories suggesting that Jews first set foot on Chinese soil during the talmudic period make sense but lack documentary support. This was the time when the Silk Road was opened as a trade route between East and West. As discussed in Chapter 1, there is a good deal of evidence that merchants and traders from places where there was a heavy Jewish presence used the Silk Road to travel to China for commercial purposes, and there were certainly Jews among them.

Brotier argues that the claim by Kaifeng Jews that their ancestors settled in China during the Han dynasty (206 B.C.E–222 C.E.) is probably reliable. Several of them, he notes, said that the Jews had come to China during the reign of Ming Ti, a ruler who ascended the throne in 58 C.E. and died in 78, and these dates concide with the revolt against Rome and the destruction of Jerusalem in 70, events that forced Jews from Palestine to wander far afield in search of a new home. [4]

This theory is entirely feasible, especially because the Silk Road was in regular use by merchants and traders from Western Asian countries, but without evidence assumptions or theories can only remain assumptions or theories.

THE TANG DYNASTY

The Tang (618–906) is the period when we begin to have documentary evidence for the presence of Jews in China. The earliest extant authentic evidence is from the beginning of the eighth century: a business letter written in Judeo-Persian, discovered by Sir Marc Aurel Stein, a Hungarian-born British Jewish orientalist and archaeologist. The Judeo-Persian letter (now housed in the British Museum) was found in Danfan Uiliq in Northwest China in 1901. The text is thirty-seven lines in length and was written on paper, a product then manufactured only in China. It was identified by David Samuel Margoliouth, an expert on Judeo-Persian studies, as dating from 718 C.E.[5]

From this fragment, we learn that a Persian-speaking Jew was trading commodities. He wrote to a fellow Jew who was obviously also a trader and asked his help in disposing of some sheep of inferior stock that he had the misfortune to own.

Another bit of authentic evidence for the presence of Jews in China is a page of Hebrew penitential prayers extracted by Paul Pelliot in 1908 from a massive trove of documents in the Cave of the Thousand Buddhas of Dunhuang, which was also collected by Stein. It consists of passages from the Psalms and the Prophets and also dates back to the eighth century.

The earliest historical references to Jews in China are by Arabic writers of the ninth and tenth centuries. Abu-Zaid, a medieval Arab geographer and traveler, described the massacre in 877 (or 878) of the foreign residents of the city of Khanfu by the Chinese rebel Banshu. Among those killed he specifically mentions Jews.[6]

Although we cannot be too certain where Khanfu was located, we do know that it was in South China.

All this evidence and more tells us that there were Jews in China no later than the Tang dynasty.

From 1280 on, a few Chinese sources also mention the Jewish presence in China. The *Statutes of the Yuan* and the *Official History of the Yuan* mention Jews several times.[7]

Westerners who were in China in this period also repeatedly mention Jews. For example, Marco Polo says there were Jews in Beijing in 1286. Olschki writes of "an organized Jewish community, which was granted official recognition." The Franciscan John of Monte Corvino notes that there were Jews in China around 1300. Andrew of Perugia mentioned Jews in China in 1326. Jean de

Marignolli asserts that he had disputes with Jews in Khanbaliq, China, in 1342. The Arab Ibn-Battuta mentions a "Jews' Gate" in Hangzhou in 1346.[8]

A good number of Jews must have gone to China for commercial and business purposes. They came from a variety of places, by whatever route seemed most expedient, traveling by land and by sea. Some went back and forth. Others stayed and eventually settled there. Inevitably, some fair-sized Jewish communities appeared in the cities where they had business and resided. Other Jews were brought to China as captives during the Mongol march of conquest through Central Asia and Eastern Europe in the thirteenth and fourteenth centuries.

Some of the Jewish communities in other cities had connections or contacts with Kaifeng Jewry, others did not.

XI'AN

Xi'an has always been the largest and most important city in Northwest China. It is also one of China's most ancient capital cities. Because of the Silk Road, it was formerly the most important center of trade in Asia. Che Muqi, a Chinese historian, says in his *The Silk Road: Past and Present*:

> Xi'an was the largest metropolis in the East . . . , rivaling Rome and Constantinople in the West. It measured 8.4 kilometers from north to south, and 9.7 kilometers from east to west, covering an area of 81.8 square kilometers. The main street (Red Bird Street) was 150 meters wide. To be compared with streets in the largest city of Roman Empire [which] were 12 meters wide at most; the streets in Athens, Greece, were only five meters wide. It certainly set a world record for ancient city construction. The city's population then was one million, a truly international metropolis.

Che Muqi vividly describes the cosmopolitan life of Xi'an. He tells us that many students from Japan and from Central and West

Asian countries studied in the imperial college there. A large number of Persians settled in the city, including Prince Peroz. Some of the foreigners were engaged in religious activities, others were merchants and traders.[9]

It is hard to imagine that no Jews ever visited or lived in Xi'an during the Tang dynasty, especially because there were so many Arab and Persian merchants and traders from the very regions where Jews were well-known as merchants and traders. Kong Xianyi believes that Xi'an had a large Jewish community in the mid-Tang dynasty. A Chinese poem written in that period mentions Jews and testifies to their presence in the city.[10]

Therefore, Xi'an is most likely one of the first Chinese cities where a fairly large number of Jews dwelled before the tenth century as well as in later periods.

BEIJING

Beijing (Peking) is a city in North China. It first became important when the Mongols took it in 1215 and made it their capital after they established the Yuan dynasty (1279–1368). Marco Polo, the first European to give a detailed account of a journey to China, arrived in Beijing, which he called Cambaluc (from the Mongol Khanbaliq, meaning "city of the ruler"), in 1275 and became a minor official at the Mongol court. He mentions that there were Jews in Beijing in 1286. He also says that the Yuan emperor showed great respect for four religions, one of which was Judaism.[11] Later travelers, such as the Franciscan Marignolli, also mentioned Jews in the city. Marignolli says he debated religious questions with them. There were still many Jews in Beijing at the end of the sixteenth century. Benedict Goes claims that he met a Muslim trader from Kashgar who told him he had encountered several "disciples of Moses" in Beijing.[12]

The *Official History of the Yuan* for 1354 says that "the skilled archers of Ningsia and wealthy Muslims (?) and Jews from various places were summoned to the capital to volunteer for military service."[13]

In 1605, Ai Tien from Kaifeng visited Beijing and met the Jesuit priest Matteo Ricci. Other Jews from Kaifeng visited the city later on. More recently, Schereschewsky met Kaifeng Jews in Beijing, and this led to his visit to Kaifeng in 1867.[14]

HANGZHOU

Hangzhou is located in East China and became prominent when the Sui dynasty (581–618) made it the southern terminus of the Grand Canal, which runs from north to south, joining several major rivers to provide China with an extensive inland waterway system. After 1126, Hangzhou served as the capital of the Southern Song dynasty. It has always been known as an important trade and handicrafts center. Its direct access to major sea routes made it convenient for merchants and traders.

Hangzhou is one of the few Chinese cities that we are sure had a Jewish community. Although the arrival of the first settlers cannot be precisely dated, it would not be unreasonable to assume the presence of a Jewish community as early as the twelfth century, when the Northern Song was defeated by the Tartars and forced to move its capital from Kaifeng to Hangzhou. Chinese documents show that a large part of Kaifeng's populace moved with the royal court. Quite likely, some of Kaifeng's Jews were among them.

Ai Tien, the Jew from Kaifeng who met Matteo Ricci in Beijing, told him that many Jews had once lived in Hangzhou, forming a large Jewish community with a synagogue of its own.[15] He did not say how he knew this (or perhaps Ricci did not mention it in his reports to Rome). Scholars assume that at least some of the Hangzhou Jews had their roots in Kaifeng and were descended from people who came to the city around 1127 when the Song court moved there from Kaifeng. Obviously, the Hangzhou and Kaifeng Jews had some kind of connection that made Ai Tien's knowledge possible.

The existence of the Hangzhou Jewish community is incidentally attested by the Arab traveler Ibn Battuta, who visited Hangzhou in 1346. When he and his companions entered the city, they immediately became aware of a Jewish presence there because of the name of the gate through which they passed. He wrote: "We entered . . . through a gate called the Jews' Gate. In this city live Jews, Christians, and some worshipping Turks, a large number in all."[16]

For some reason, the Jewish community of Hangzhou ceased to exist sometime before the seventeenth century.

NINGPO

Ningpo has been a seaport in East China for many centuries. Before modern times, it was the most important port connecting that part of China to Southeast Asia and beyond. It was one of the five treaty ports opened to foreign trade in 1842. The presence of Jews seems likely, for as is pointed out by Paul Pelliot:

> At Ningbo, as in all this region of the estuary of the Yangtse, adventurers and merchants from the large Persian junks, people of all races and creeds, Manichaeans and Mazdeans, Muslims and Nestorians, bumped into brethren coming by the other route, via Turkestan and Kansu. It would be strange if the Jews were the only ones who remained outside this stream.[17]

In fact, the Jewish presence in the city began early. The Ningpo Jews established ties with Kaifeng Jewry by the fifteenth century if not before. In 1461, the Jews in Kaifeng obtained two Torah scrolls from Ningpo. The 1489 inscription tells the story:

> . . . when the synagogue was rebuilt, Shi Bin, Li Rong, and Gao Jian, and Zhang Xuan went to Ningpo and brought back a scroll of the Scriptures. Zhao Ying of Ningpo brought another scroll to Kaifeng and respectfully presented it to our temple.

From this it may be deduced that there was a fairly large Jewish community in Ningpo. They must have had many more Torah scrolls if they could spare two for the Jews of Kaifeng.

Pan Guandan believes that the Jews in Ningpo probably arrived very early because it is a river port quite near the sea. The fact that they had many Torah scrolls "indicates that the Jews and Judaism of Ningpo probably had a history no shorter than their Kaifeng counterparts, plus a considerable prestige."[18]

The existence of the Ningpo Jewish community gave support, at least spiritually, to the Kaifeng Jewish community. The Torah scrolls it sent certainly provided means for the Kaifeng Jews to hold together in their ritual and education.

YANGZHOU

Yangzhou was originally a seaport. In the seventh to ninth centuries, as the course of the Yangtze River changed and its delta extended farther into the ocean, Yangzhou became a river port. Because of its location on the Grand Canal, Yangzhou became an important hub from which one could travel south to Fujian and Canton and north to Kaifeng. Zhu Jiang, a Chinese historian, describes its ties with Kaifeng:

> Yangzhou was directly connected with the capital on Kaifeng by the Grand Canal, which greatly facilitated trade and the transport of goods, a fact well known to the West Asians. Korean emissaries and merchants, whose country was much nearer, preferred sailing down to Yangzhou and then up the Grand Canal to the overland road across the Shangtong Peninsula. Traders and emissaries from West Asia had even more reason to consider this the quickest, safest, and cheapest way to trade and transport merchandise to and from Kaifeng. Jews sailing to China from Bombay would, of necessity, first have to land in Yangzhou before they could go up the Grand Canal to the nation's capital. This is what brought so many Jews to Yangzhou.[19]

There was also a very large Muslim community in the city. According to the *Fujian Chronicles*, Western Region Notes, the

Islamic religion was transmitted to Yangzhou thirteen centuries ago. Today, the Muslim population of the city numbers about four thousand. Zhu suggests that the Kaifeng Jews first came to Yangzhou by sea and then moved on to Kaifeng.[20]

It is reasonable to assume that there was a Jewish community in Yangzhou. The 1512 inscription describes the connection between Kaifeng Jewry and the Yangzhou Jews, for it states that An, Li, and Gao of Kaifeng, and Jin Pu of Yangzhou "contributed a scroll of the Torah and constructed a second gateway of the synagogue." In fact, the 1512 inscription was written by Zhu Tang, who was a resident of Yangzhou. Leslie believes that there was an established Jewish community in Yangzhou (he calls it Yangchow) and that the 1512 inscription was written there.[21]

Ai Tien, who met Ricci in Beijing, was appointed to school supervisor in Paoying District of Yangzhou for 1605–1607 according to the *Yangzhou Gazetteers*.[22] Therefore, he was in Yangzhou at least for a short time in the early seventeenth century.

NINGXIA

Ningxia is situated in Northwest China and is an important post city in that region. It too had Jewish residents. The 1489 and 1512 inscriptions testify to their existence and their connection with Kaifeng Jewry. The 1489 inscription tells how Jin Xuan, a native of Ningxia, contributed an altar, a bronze censer, vases, and candlesticks to the Kaifeng synagogue when it was rebuilt after a flood. His younger brother, Jin Ying, contributed to the funds used to purchase land for the synagogue and pay for inscribing and erecting the 1489 stele. The 1512 inscription states that Jin Run built the kiosk in which it was housed. All three Jins were from Ningxia. The 1489 inscription also mentions that one of the ancestors of Jin Xuan and Jin Ying had been court president of state banquets, and that their great-uncle had been a ranking military officer. Apparently, the Jin family had a long history in that city and kept close ties with Kaifeng Jewry. Ningxia is located on the Silk Road and served as a way-station. Merchants or traders who wanted to enter China from Central Asia via the Silk Road had to pass it. This makes the existence of Jews in the city even more probable.

CANTON

Canton is located in South China and has been a trading port for well over fifteen hundred years. Its location on the extreme southern coast makes it the Chinese port most accessible to Southeast Asia and beyond. Trade was conducted with India, Southeast Asia, Persia, and the Arab world. Arab traders, who were long dominant in Asian waters, settled there during the Tang dynasty. A mosque said to have been built in 627 by an uncle of Muhammad remains a prominent Canton landmark to this day. There was a very large Muslim community in the city for many centuries.

Canton is one of a few cities that had a large number of Jews but no proven connection with Kaifeng. Because of its importance as a seaport, starting in the Tang dynasty, merchants and traders, especially from West Asian countries, came to the city for business purposes. Quite likely there was a substantial community of Jews in this period.

The Arab traveler Abu Zaid wrote in his book that Jews were among the many victims of the peasant rebels who in 878 attacked the city of Khanfu, which many scholars believe to have been Canton.[23]

QUANZHOU

Located in southeastern Fujian Province, Quanzhou is the city referred to as Zaitun by Marco Polo. It was an important center for foreign trade during the Southern Song (1127–79) and Yuan dynasties. The city was known for the production and distribution of satin textiles, and in fact it is from the word *zaitun* that the English "satin" is derived.

The testimony to the existence of Quanzhou Jewry is a letter written by Andrew of Perugia, the city's Catholic bishop. Andrew wrote to his superior in Rome in 1326, complaining: "We are able to preach freely and unmolested, but of the Jews and Saracens [Muslims] none is converted."[24] Given the city's economic role and its many contacts with outsiders, it is quite reasonable to assume the presence of Jews there at least in certain periods.

NANJING

Nanjing is situated on the southern bank of the Yangtze, the longest river in China as well as in Asia, approximately 300 kilometers from its mouth. It has been a major administrative and military center of South China ever since the fall of the Han dynasty in 220. In 1368, when the Ming dynasty was formally established and Nanjing became the capital, its population increased and so did its importance.

Toward the end of the Ming, Alvare de Semmedo, a Portuguese Jesuit, met a Muslim in Nanjing and was told that there had been four Jewish families living in the city but all had recently converted to Islam. Since these four families were said to have been the last of the city's Jews, there must once have been others.[25]

SHANGHAI

One Chinese city had a fairly large Jewish population in modern times, numbering about thirty thousand. The Jewish presence in Shanghai began in the 1840s, and is a topic beyond the scope of this book, but the city's Jews nonetheless deserve some mention because of their contacts with Kaifeng Jewry.

Shanghai became an important city after 1842 when the British defeated China in the so-called Opium Wars and forced the emperor to open five treaty ports to merchants from the West. Because of its geographic location, Shanghai grew very fast and soon became China's most important port. Jews from outside of China came to the city on business in 1844 and established a community of their own shortly after. The first Jewish cemetery in Shanghai was established in 1862, and the first synagogue in 1887.

Two Jews from Kaifeng visited Shanghai as early as 1851, in company with some Jesuit missionaries they had met in Kaifeng. Although this visit had nothing to do with the Shanghai Jewish community, which did not exist at the time, it tells us there was a connection of some kind with the city.

By the end of the nineteenth century, a Shanghai Jewish community of Sephardic origin had not only taken shape, but become well-established. Worried by reports about the tragic situation of Kaifeng Jewry, the Jews of Shanghai took on the responsibility of extending a helping hand. On March 13, 1900, a letter signed by forty-six Shanghai Jews was sent to Kaifeng to express affection and support. It reads:

We address you, brethren in faith, having heard that in days gone by you had a synagogue at Kai-fung-foo, and ministers who taught you the ordinances and laws, how to worship the Lord God of Israel. We now learn that your House of Worship is destroyed, and that you have no Rabbi or teacher to instruct you and to show you the way wherein you should walk as prescribed by the law of Moses and as we are exhorted by the prophets and Ezra the scribe.

We are told that you have forgotten everything, and have gone so far as, three or four months ago, to have sold a scroll of the Law, which our own eyes have seen in the hands of those that are not of the seed of Israel. And we are further told that you are about to dispose of three or four more scrolls because you are in dire distress, and urge as your excuse that you and your children cannot read.

Now, verily, sorrow and anxiety filled our hearts when we heard these evil tidings, that affliction and want have brought you to this pass, so that Sabbath and festivals are forgotten, and that you are becoming mixed up with the heathen around you, and that you forsake the covenant, and the way your forefathers have walked for 2000 years in this land of your settlement. Tidings such as these caused the ears of every one of us that heard to tingle, and we have roused ourselves to come to your help.

Some of us were willing to come to you to find out where-fore all this evil has befallen you, and to see what we could do to heal the breach. But we are told that there would be dan-ger to us on the way, and excite the Gentiles among whom you dwell, therefore we decided to write to you this epistle, and to ask you to send us an answer, either by letter or by word of mouth, through a member of your community.

Now, we assure you that we are eager to help you accord-ing to our ability, so that you may walk again in the footsteps of your forefathers. If you desire to rebuild the House of God, which has now become a wasted place, we will collect money and send it to you; if you want a teacher to instruct you, we will send you one; if it should please you to come hither and settle here in the city of Shanghai, we will help you to do so, and put you in the way to earn a livelihood by starting you in a trade, and all that you may require; in this city are men of our faith—great and wealthy men of affairs and business—who can help you to maintain yourselves and your sons and daughters.

Therefore we beg you not to part with the scrolls still left to you. On this letter reaching you, send two or three men to us whom we may question, and from whom we can find out what we can do for you. We will pay all the expenses of the messengers; we will give them their sustenance, and pay them their expenses until they reach again your city.[26]

The letter concluded with a suggestion that the Jews of Kaifeng send a representative to Shanghai to enumerate their needs. The Kaifeng Jews excitedly selected Li Jingsheng as their emissary. Li, a flour merchant, went to Shanghai and was warmly received. David Ezekiel Abraham, one of the best-known leaders of Shanghai's Sephardic community, became his host, happy to provide him with board and lodging.

After three weeks, Li returned to Kaifeng to report back to his colleagues. Anticipating financial aid from Shanghai, they began planning to rebuild the synagogue and reestablish a formally orga-nized Jewish community. But none of this came to pass. Despite their promises, the Shanghai Jews provided little monetary assistance, and without it the Kaifeng Jews were powerless.

As evidence of their sincerity and to better present themselves, the Jews of Shanghai set up the Society for the Rescue of the Chinese Jews on May 14, 1900. One of its objectives was "to bring back to Judaism all Chinese Jews linearly descended from Jewish families."[27]

The following year, another delegation set out from Kaifeng for Shanghai. The Shanghai Jewish community tried diligently to provide the Kaifeng Jews with support and help, calling upon world Jewry for assistance. Unfortunately, world Jewry had other concerns. The wave of pogroms spreading through Russia and the critical situation of the Jews in other East European countries had precipitated a vast flow of refugees, whose needs exhausted its resources, and in consequence it failed to respond. Only Shanghai was in position to aid the orphan Kaifeng colony. Shanghai's Jewish leaders promised employment with one of the city's Jewish firms, such as E. D. Sassoon & Co., to anyone from Kaifeng who chose to come.

Li and his son remained in Shanghai. Li died of illness in 1903 and was buried in one of the city's Jewish cemeteries. When his body was prepared for burial, it was discovered that he had been circumcised. His son, Li Shumei, was circumcised in Shanghai and worked and lived there until 1945, when he finally decided to return to Kaifeng.[28]

Besides the above-mentioned places, there may have been Jews, at one time or another, in several other Chinese cities, such as Luoyang, Dunhuang, and Nanchang, as well as the provinces of Yunnan and Xingjiang. However, by the seventeenth century, all these other Jewish communities seem to have disappeared, including the community of Hangzhou, even though individuals may occasionally have lingered for a while. When Ai Tien met Ricci in Beijing in 1605, he told him that there were no other Jews in China. We do not know what happened to the other Jewish communities. They simply were no longer there. Obviously, the Jews of these communities must have been assimilated into the vast populace of China. Moreover, all our knowledge of a Jewish presence in the other cities comes from cross-references. Not one of them left any record of its existence, or at least none has yet been found.

The only Jewish community that survived in China is the one in Kaifeng. This phenomenon inevitably raises a question: What made it possible for the Kaifeng community to survive for at least eight hundred consecutive years while all the others vanished? The answer lies in the uniqueness of the Kaifeng Jewish community. Perhaps this book has provided part, if not all, of the answer.

[1] In biblical Hebrew Sinim may refer to China. Because of this, some scholars believe that there were Jews in China in Isaiah's time.

[2] Pollak, Mandarins, Jews, and Missionaries, p. 256.

[3] Rabinowitz, Jewish Merchant Adventurers, p. 65.

[4] White, Chinese Jews, pt. I, p. 66.

[5] For details, see Margoliouth, "An Early Judaeo-Persian Document in the Stern Collection."

[6] Leslie, Survival of the Chinese Jews, pp. 7–8.

[7] Ibid., pp. 12–15.

[8] Ibid., p. 15.

[9] Che Muqi, Silk Road, Past and Present, pp. 30–31.

[10] Kong Xianyi, "Delving into the Kaifeng Israelite Religion."

[11] See Adler, Jewish Travellers, pp. 6–7.

[12] Cf. Shapiro, Jews in Old China, p. 103.

[13] Leslie, Survival of the Chinese Jews, p. 13.

[14] Ibid., p. 193.

[15] Gallagher, China in the Sixteenth Century, p. 108.

[16] Ibid., p. 15.

[17] Leslie, "Kaifeng Jewish Community," p. 188.

[18] Cf. Shapiro, Jews in Old China, p. 63.

[19] Ibid., p. 145.

[20] Zhu Jiang, "Jewish Traces in Yangzhou." In Shapiro, Jews in Old China, pp. 143–158.

[21] Leslie, Survival of the Chinese Jews, p. 30.

[22] Yangzhou Gazetteers, 1810, 37, p. 5 Ia. Cf. Leslie, Survival of the Chinese Jews, p. 203.

[23] Cf. Leslie, *Survival of the Chinese Jews*, p. 7.

[24] Cf. Shapiro, *Jews in Old China*, p. 64.

[25] Ibid.

[26] Adler, "Chinese Jews," in Kublin, *Jews in Old China*, pp. 116–117.

[27] White, *Chinese Jews*, pt. I, p. 152.

[28] Wang Yisha, *Spring and Autumn of the Chinese Jews*, pp. 189–191.

Bibliography

Abraham, Wendy. "Memories of Kaifeng's Jewish Descendants Today: Historical Significance in Light of Observations by Westerners Since 1605." Paper read at the International Conference on "Jews in China: A Comparative and Historical Perspective." Harvard University, 1992.

Adler, Elkan N. *Jewish Travellers*. London: Routledge, 1930.

Adler, Marcus N. "Chinese Jews." *Jewish Quarterly Review*. 1900.

Broomhall, Marshall B. *Islam in China*. New York, 1966.

Brown, David A. "Brown Rediscovers China's Ancient Jews." *American Hebrew and Jewish Tribune*, January 27–March 10, 1933.

Che Muqi. *The Silk Road, Past and Present*. Beijing: Foreign Languages Press, 1989.

Chen Changqi. "Some Questions Regarding the History of the Kaifeng Jews." Zhengzhou, 1983.

Chen Yuan. "A Study of the Israelite Religion in Kaifeng" (1920). In *The Academic Theses of Chen Yuan*. Vol. 1. Beijing: Zhonghua Shuju, 1980.

Dehergne, Joseph, and Donald D. Leslie. *Juifs de Chine*. Rome: Institutum Historicum S.I., 1980.

Dien, Albert, ed. *Sino-Judaica: Occasional Papers of the Sino-Judaic Institute.*

Drenger, B. D., ed. *The Haggadah of the Chinese Jews.* New York: Orphan Hospital Ward of Israel, 1967.

Eban, Abba. *Heritage: Civilization and the Jews.* New York: Summit Books, 1984.

Eber, Irene. "Yehudei Kaifeng: Hitarut be-tarbut Sin u-deveikut ba-zehut ha-Yehudit." *Pe'amim* 41 (Autumn 1989).

Embree, Ainslie T., ed. *Encyclopedia of Asian History.* New York: Charles Scribner's Sons and Collier Macmillan, 1988.

Ezra, Edward I. "Chinese Jews." *East of Asia Magazine.* 1902.

───── and Arthur Sopher. "Chinese Jews." Shanghai, 1926. In Kublin, *Jews in Old China.*

Fink, Aaron Halevy. "Jews in China." *Jewish Chronicle*, February 7, 14, and 21, 1868.

Finn, James. *The Jews in China: Their Synagogue, Their Scriptures, Their History, &c.* London: B. Wertheim, Aldin Chambers, 1853.

─────. *The Orphan Colony of the Jews in China.* 1872.

Friend, Beverly. "A Visit to Kaifeng." *Humanistic Judaism* 23, nos. 3–4, p. 37.

Gallagher, Louis J., trans. *China in the Sixteenth Century: The Journals of Matthew Ricci, 1583–1610.* New York: Random House, 1953.

Gao Wangzi. "The Assimilation of the Chinese Jews." In *East Gate of Kaifeng: A Jewish World Inside China*. Edited by M. Patricia Needle. Minneapolis: China Center, University of Minnesota, 1992.

Gernet, Jacques. *A History of Chinese Civilization*. Trans. J. R. Foster. Cambridge: Cambridge University Press, 1982.

Gilbert, Martin. *The Atlas of Jewish History*. New York: Dorset Press, 1984.

Gong Fangzhen. "The Jewish Merchants on the Silk Road." Paper read at the International Conference on "Jews in China: A Comparative and History Perspective." Harvard University, 1992.

Har-El, Menashe. In *Ariel*, no. 84 (1991).

Holm, Frits. *My Nestorian Adventure in China*. New York: Fleming H. Revell, 1923.

Israel, Benjamin J. *The Jews of India*. New Delhi: Centre for Jewish and Inter-Faith Studies, Jewish Welfare Association, 1982.

Jewish Encyclopedia. New York: Funk & Wagnalls, 1906–7.

Jiang Qingxiang and Xiao Guoliang. "Glimpses of the Urban Economy of Bianjing, Capital of the Northern Song Dynasty as Seen in the Painting *Riverside Scene at Clear and Bright Festival Time* and the Book *Reminiscences of Dreamland Glories of the Eastern Capital*." *Social Sciences in China* 4 (1981).

Jin Xiaojing. "I Am a Chinese Jew." *Universal Knowledge Quarterly* 4 (1981).

Katz, Nathan. "The Judaism of Kaifeng and Cochin: Parallel and Divergent Styles of Religious Acculturation." *Numen* 42 (1995).

Kong Xianyi. "Delving into the Kaifeng Israelite Religion." *Materials on World Religions*, no. 2 (1986), pp. 5–13.

Kramer, Lawrence. "The K'aifeng Jews: A Disappearing Community. In *Studies of the Chinese Jews*, compiled by Hyman Kublin.

Kublin, Hyman, comp. *Jews in Old China*. New York: Paragon Books, 1971.

―――, comp. *Studies of the Chinese Jews: Selections from Journals East and West*. New York: Paragon Books, 1971.

Laufer, Berthold. "A Chinese-Hebrew Manuscript: A New Source for the History of the Chinese Jews." In Kublin, *Studies of the Chinese Jews*.

Leslie, Donald D. *The Chinese-Hebrew Memorial Book of the Jewish Community of Kaifeng*. Belconnen, A.C.T.: Canberra College of Advanced Education, 1984.

―――. "Integration, Assimilation and Survival of Minorities in China: The Case of the Kaifeng Jews." Paper read at the International Colloquium "From Kaifeng to Shanghai: Jews in China." Sankt Augustin, Germany, September 22–26, 1997.

―――. "The K'aifeng Jew Chao Ying-ch'eng and His Family." In Kublin, *Studies of the Chinese Jews*.

―――. "The Kaifeng Jewish Community: A Summary." *Jewish Journal of Sociology* 2 (1969). Also in Kublin, *Studies of the Chinese Jews*.

————. *The Survival of the Chinese Jews*. Leiden: E. J. Brill, 1975.

———— and Maisie Meyer. "The Shanghai Society for the Rescue of the Chinese Jews." In *Sino-Judaica: Occasional Papers of the Sino-Judaic Institute*, ed. Albert Dien, vol. 2 (1985), pp. 47–66.

Li Ung Bing. *Outlines of Chinese History*. Shanghai: Commercial Press, 1914.

Loewenthal, Rudolf. "The Early Jews in China: A Supplementary Bibliography." 1946.

————. "The Jews in China: A Bibliography." 1939.

Mandelbaum, David G., ed. *Selected Writings of Edward Sapir*. Berkeley: University of California Press, 1949.

Margoliouth, David S. "An Early Judaeo-Persian Document from Khotan in the Stein Collection, with Other Early Persian Documents." *Journal of the Royal Asiatic Society of Great Britain and Ireland* 55 (1903): 735–760.

Martin, W. A. P. "Account of a Visit to the Jews in Honan." 1881.

————. "Jews in China." *Jewish Times* (New York), March 26, 1869, p. 5.

Mendelssohn, Sidney. *The Jews of Asia*. London: Kegan Paul, Trench, Trubner & Co., and E. P. Dutton, 1920.

Meskill, John, ed. *An Introduction to Chinese Civilization*. New York: Columbia University Press, 1973.

Modrzejewski, Joseph Meleze. *The Jews of Egypt*. Trans. Robert Cornman. Philadelphia: Jewish Publication Society, 1995.

Norollah, M. "The Jews in China." J(M)I October 1896, p. 7.

Pan Guangdan. *Jews in Ancient China: A Historical Survey.* With a preface by Wu Zhelin. Peking University Press, 1983.

Perlmann, "The History of the Jews in China." In Kublin, *Jews in Old China*

Plaks, Andrew. "The Confucianization of the Chinese Jews: Interpretations of the Kaifeng Stelae Inscriptions." In *East Gate of Kaifeng: A Jewish World Inside China.* Edited by M. Patricia Needle. University of Minnesota China Center, 1992.

Pollak, Michael. *The Jews of Dynastic China: A Critical Bibliography.* Cincinnati: Hebrew Union College Press and Sino-Judaic Institute, 1993.

————. *Mandarins, Jews, and Missionaries.* Philadelphia: Jewish Publication Society, 1980.

————. *The Torah Scrolls of the Chinese Jews: The History, Significance and Present Whereabouts of the Sifrei Torah of the Defunct Jewish Community of Kaifeng.* Dallas: Bridwell Library, Southern Methodist University, 1975.

Rabinowitz, L. *Jewish Merchant Adventurers: A Study of the Radanites.* London: Edward Goldston, 1948.

Rossabi, Morris. "Muslims and Central Asian Revolts in Late Ming and Early Ch'ing." In *From Ming to Ch'ing: Conquest, Region and Continuity in Seventeenth-Century China.* Edited by Jonathan D. Spence and John E. Wills, Jr. New Haven: Yale University Press, 1979.

Shapiro, Sidney, trans. and ed. *Jews in Old China: Studies by Chinese Scholars*. New York: Hippocrene Books, 1984.

Shi Jingxun. Article in *Sino-Judaica*, ed. Albert Dien, vol. 1 (1990).

Smith, George. *The Jews at K'ae-fung-foo: Being a Narrative of a Mission of Inquiry to the Jewish Synagogue at K'ae-fung-goo on Behalf of the London Society for Promoting Christianity Among the Jews*. London, 1851.

Trustch, Matthew, and Jonathan Shulman. "Minyan in Kaifeng: What Is a Jew?" *China/Judaic Connection* 7, no. 1 (Winter 1998).

Wang Yisha. *Spring and Autumn of the Chinese Jews*. Ocean Press, 1984.

Weinryb, Bernard D. *The Jews of Poland*. Philadelphia: Jewish Publication Society, 1982.

White, William C. *Chinese Jews*. Toronto: University of Toronto Press, 1942.

Wigoder, Geoffrey, ed. *The Encyclopedia of Judaism*. Jerusalem: Jerusalem Publishing House, 1989.

Wu Zhelin. Preface to *Jews in Ancient China: A Historical Survey*, by Pan Guandan. Peking University Press, 1983.

Xu Xin, with Beverly Friend. *Legends of the Chinese Jews of Kaifeng*. Hoboken, N.J.: KTAV Publishing House, 1995.

____ and Lin Jiyao, eds. *Encyclopaedia Judaica* (in Chinese). Shanghai: Shanghai People's Publishing House, 1993.

Zhao Xiangruo. Paper read at the International Conference on "Jews in China: A Comparative and Historical Perspective." Harvard University, 1992.

Zhu Jiang. "Jewish Traces in Yangzhou." Yangzhou, 1983.

Chronological Table

960–1279 The Song dynasty. Northern Song period (960–1126), with Kaifeng as its capital; Southern Song period (1127–1279), with Hangzhou as its capital, after defeat by the Tartars.

960–1126 Jews of Persian origin settled in Kaifeng.

1163 The Kaifeng Jews constructed a synagogue building, the first in China. The site remained in their possession until 1914.

1279 The synagogue was rebuilt during the reign of Yuan emperor Kublai Khan. It was named "Ancient Temple of Purity and Truth."

1280 References to Jews, although not necessarily the Kaifeng Jews, begin to appear in Chinese sources, such as *Statutes of the Yuan* and *Official History of the Yuan*. They mention marriage practices, ritual slaughter, and other Jewish customs.

1286 Marco Polo, in China from 1275 to 1292 serving Yuan court, met Jews in Peking.

1421–23 An San, a Kaifeng Jew, became assistant commissioner of the Embroidered Uniform Guard and received the new surname Zhao. Perhaps the first Jew to become a ranking Chinese official, he earned a place in the records of the Ming dynasty.

1421   The synagogue underwent a major reconstruction spon-
          sored by the prince of Zhou. In gratitude to the Ming
          authorities, an imperial tablet was placed in the syna-
          gogue.

1426–36   Kao Nien, a Kaifeng Jew, obtained the title of *Kung
          Sheng.*

1436   Kao Nien was appointed a magistrate and occupied this
          post in County She of Anhui Province until 1450.

1445   The synagogue was renovated. Several buildings were
          added to the synagogue compound.

1447   Ai Chun obtained the title of *Ju Ren* after passing the
          imperial examinations.

1461   The synagogue was repaired and enlarged after a Yellow
          River flood. the Rear Hall was added, and on the out-
          side, a corridor connecting with the Front Hall. New
          copies of the Law were procured.

1457   Two Torah scrolls were brought to Kaifeng from
          Ningpo.

1465–88   A Hall of Scriptures was added to the synagogue com-
          pound.

1489   The synagogue was rebuilt. The 1489 inscription, the
          first stele erected by the Kaifeng community, provides a
          history of Kaifeng Jewry and is still extant.

1512   The synagogue was repaired. The 1512 stele, also still
          extant, was erected.

1573   Ai Tien passed a provincial examination and became *Ju Ren*. He served as supervisor of schools from 1605 to 1608 in Paoying District of Yangzhou, Jiangsu Province.

1605   Ai Tien met Fr. Matteo Ricci in Peking, and as a result Kaifeng Jewry became known worldwide. *China in the Sixteenth Century*, by Louis J. Gallagher, published later, gives a full account of the meeting and Ricci's reaction.

1608   Fr. Ricci sent two Chinese Christians to visit Kaifeng with a letter to the chief rabbi. Three Kaifeng Jews, in turn, visited him in Peking.

1613   Fr. Jules Aleni, an Italian Jesuit, visited Kaifeng and asked to see the Torah scrolls, but permission was not granted.

1615   Li Chen obtained his *Ju Ren* title and was appointed district magistrate.

1640   Fr. Figueredo, a Portuguese Jesuit, lived in Kaifeng and had contacts with the city's Jews. He was drowned in the 1642 flood.

1642   The worst Yellow River flood in 1,000 years destroyed most of Kaifeng and killed about two-thirds of its populace. The synagogue was completely destroyed, but about 200 Jewish families survived.

1644   Fr. Enriquez, another Jesuit, lived in Kaifeng for some years and visited the synagogue.

1644–62   Ai Ying-kuei, a Jew, served as an official physician to the prince of Zhou.

1645   Zhao Yingcheng obtained the *Ju Ren*. In 1646, he
            became a *Jing Shi*, the highest rank ever obtained by a
            Kaifeng Jew, and was appointed surveillance vice-com-
            missioner, serving in Fujian and Huguang Provinces.

ca. 1650   *Ju-meng-lu*, a book by a Chinese writer, mentioned the
            synagogue of the Kaifeng Jewish community.

1652   Kao Xuan obtained the title of *Kung Sheng*.

1653   Zhao Yingdou obtained his *Kung Sheng*.

1653   The rebuilding of the synagogue commenced.

1663   The dedication of the reconstructed synagogue
            (destroyed in the 1642 flood). The stele is no longer
            extant, but the text has survived.

ca. 1670   The Chinese-Hebrew Memorial Book of the Jewish
            Community of Kaifeng was closed.

1679   The synagogue was further repaired. A stele was dedi-
            cated by the Zhao clan but remained unknown until
            1905, when it was found by Edward Jenks, an American
            engineer.

1687   Zhao Wenbin obtained his military *Ju Ren* title.

1688   The synagogue was renovated. Many vertical plaques
            were dedicated. This was apparently the last time the
            synagogue was repaired or renovated.

1695   Zhao Yingkun served as assistant editor of the Kaifeng-
            fu gazetteer.

1698   Fr. Jean-Paul Gozani, an Italian Jesuit, lived in Kaifeng off and on for over twenty years. He tried to visit the Kaifeng Jewish community in 1701, but was unable to do so until 1704, reporting his findings in a letter to Rome on November 5. He autographed a single page of Hebrew and Latin, which lists the names of books of the Talmud. He was the first person to make rubbings of the Chinese inscriptions in the synagogue.

1705   Fr. Phillippe Grimaldi, director of the Board of Mathematics at Peking and rector of the Italian Jesuits at the beginning of the eighteenth century, signed and sealed a manuscript copy of seven tablet inscriptions from the synagogue on November 8.

1721–22 Fr. Jean Domenge, a French Jesuit, visited Kaifeng twice and had close contacts with its Jews. He wrote six letters from 1721–25. He made drawings of the congregational Torah reading and the interior and exterior of the synagogue, and gave a basic account of the books of the Bible and other Hebrew books held by the Kaifeng Jews. He also copied a Judeo-Persian colophon to the Pentateuch and provided information about festival celebrations and the pronunciation of Hebrew.

1723   Fr. Antoine Gaubil, a French Jesuit, visited Kaifeng in March. His brief summaries of four inscriptions in Chinese were the first real account of the stelae and their contents. His *Correspondance de Pekin* (1722–59, republished 1970) makes many references to his visit to Kaifeng.

1723   Yung-cheng, an emperor of the Qing dynasty, expelled missionaries from China, isolating it from the rest of the world. The Kaifeng Jews were once again cut off from contacts with Jews in other countries.

1724   Fr. Gozani was expelled from Kaifeng.

1770   Fr. Pierre Cibot, a French Jesuit, published a memoir on
            the Jews in China.

1771   Abbé Gabriel Brotier published a memoir on the Jews
            in China, based on the letters of Gozani (1704), Gaubil
            (1723), and Domenge (1722). The memoir was com-
            piled in 1770 and included Domenge's sketches of the
            synagogue.

1795   Alexander Hirsch and Solomon Joseph Simson wrote a
            letter in Hebrew to the Kaifeng Jews, inquiring about
            the welfare of the community and asking for informa-
            tion about its history, religious practices, and holy
            books. The letter was not delivered and was returned to
            them.

1806   Fr. Ignaz Kogler, a German Jesuit and superior of the
            Catholic Mission in China and Japan, published an
            account of the Chinese Jews with a bibliography.

1841   A major Yellow River flood struck Kaifeng. Many resi-
            dents were killed.

1843   James Finn published The Jews in China.

1850   A letter on behalf of Kaifeng Jewry, dated August 20
            and signed by Chao Nien-tsu, was sent to T. H. Layton,
            British consul in Amoy, in response to an inquiry from
            James Finn. The letter, which did not reach its
            addressee until April 1870, provides the only first-hand
            information about the community since the beginning
            of the nineteenth century.

1850   Two Chinese Protestants, Qiu Tiansheng and Jiang
              Rongji, visited the Jewish community of Kaifeng on
              December 9–14. While there they purchased eight
              Hebrew manuscripts. Their journals were published in
              1851 by Bishop George Smith of Hong Kong in his *The
              Jews at K'ae-fung-foo* on behalf of the London Society
              for Promoting Christianity Among the Jews.

1851   The two Chinese Christians visited Kaifeng again. On
              their return to Shanghai they brought along six Torah
              scrolls and fifty or sixty Hebrew manuscripts in addition
              to the Chinese-Hebrew Memorial Book of the Dead.
              Two Kaifeng Jews, Zhao Wenkui and Zhao Jincheng,
              accompanied them to Shanghai.

1850–64   The Taiping rebellion. Many Jews as well as other resi-
              dents fled from Kaifeng when the rebels marched on the
              city. Quite a few Jews never returned.

1855–78   Muslim rebellions broke out in various parts of China
              and were severely suppressed. Many Kaifeng Jews, fear-
              ing they might be persecuted because many Chinese
              associated them with the Muslims, chiseled their family
              names off the stelae.

1860   Another Yellow River flood struck Kaifeng.

1860s   The Kaifeng Jewish community came to an end. Its his-
              tory and tradition survive mainly in the memories of
              those individuals who consider themselves Jewish
              descendants.

1866   Rev. W. A. P. Martin, visited Kaifeng on February 17
              and found that the synagogue no longer existed; its site
              was an open space, with only a stele bearing the 1489

and 1512 inscriptions still standing. His visit resulted in an article entitled "Account of a Visit to the Jews in Honan," published in 1881.

1867   Bishop Samuel Schereschewsky, a Jewish convert to Christianity, visited Kaifeng from Peking. He stayed there for about 25 days. He met some Kaifeng Jews in Peking too.

1867   J. L. Liebermann, a Jew from the West, visited Kaifeng in July and spent ten days there. He wrote letter(s) in Hebrew to his father to report his visit.

1872   James Finn published another book called *The Orphan Colony of the Jews in China*.

1879   Jacob Liebermann, an Austrian merchant, visited Kaifeng and reported that "by order of the Government, Scrolls of the Law were exhibited in the open market place, and an advertisement in Chinese was inscribed by the side, offering a reward and leading position to anyone who would be able to explain the wording of the Scroll."

1890   Rev. Dennis Mills visited Kaifeng for two days. He had some conversations with local Jews. His article about this visit was published the following year.

1893   A. S. Annaud, while in Kaifeng for a few days, visited the site of the synagogue.

1899   Jesuits reportedly bought a Torah scroll and took it to Shanghai.

1900   Marcus Adler's "Chinese Jews," a lecture delivered at the Jews' College Literary Society, London, was published in the *Jewish Quarterly Review*.

1900   Fr. Jerome Tobar published at Shanghai a monograph dealing with the inscriptions of the synagogue.

1900   Rev. R. Powell visited Kaifeng in June. He sent a letter to S. J. Solomon, a Shanghai Jew.

1900   The Society for the Rescue of the Chinese Jews was founded on May 14 by Shanghai Jews. It sent some messages through Protestant missionaries, and on October 24 received a reply from Li Ching-sheng, a Kaifeng Jew and flour dealer.

1901   Sir Marc Aurel Stein, a scholar-explorer, found at the site of Khotan at Dandan-Uiliq, Turkestan, China, a mutilated Persian document, written in Hebrew letters, which was identified by D. S. Margoliouth as a business letter written around the year 718.

1901   Li Ching-sheng visited the Shanghai Jews with his 12-year-old son Li Tsung-mai on April 6. They stayed for three weeks and then returned to Kaifeng.

1902   A delegation of seven from Kaifeng came to Shanghai on March 10. Li Trung-mai was circumcised on May 27 in the house of D. E. J. Abraham and given the Hebrew name "Israel." He remained in Shanghai until 1945.

1902   Edward Isaac Ezra, a key member of the Society for the Rescue of the Chinese Jews, interviewed a group of Kaifeng Jews in his home and wrote "Chinese Jews," an article published in *East of Asia* Magazine. It appeared in 1926 with additional information added by Arthur Sopger, his brother-in-law.

1904   Edward Jenks, an American engineer, visited Kaifeng and found the 1679 inscription out of the wall of a Zhao family.

1904   Frits Holm visited Kaifeng in August. He published *My Nestorian Adventure in China* in 1923.

1905   Ph. Berthelot, a French diplomat, visited Kaifeng and met the heads of six of the seven clans.

1906   Oliver Bainbridge visited Kaifeng and mentioned that there were eight Jewish families with fifty persons.

1908   Paul Pelliot extracted a page of Hebrew penitential prayers from a massive trove of documents in the Caves of the Thousand Buddhas of Dunhuang that was originally collected by Stein. It consists of passages from the Psalms and the Prophets and dated back to the eighth century.

1908   Count Carl Gustaf Emil Mannerheim visited Kaifeng in June. He kept a diary telling of his meeting with several Jews there. He also took a photograph of a Kaifeng Jew.

1910   Zhang Xiangwen, a Chinese scholar, visited Kaifeng and met a Jew named Zhao and his nephew. Afterwards, he recounted this visit in his article, "An Early Chinese Source on the Kaifeng Jewish Community."

1910–35 The Canadian Anglican Mission began its activities in Kaifeng with Bishop William Charles White as its head. White served there until 1933, when he retired. He had many personal contacts with Kaifeng Jews and collected a large amount of data and artifacts from them. His book *Chinese Jews*, published by the University of Toronto Press in 1942, provides a handy source for the study of Kaifeng Jewry.

1912   The Canadian Anglican Mission took over protection of the two extant stelae and moved them to the cathedral compound in Kaifeng.

1914   Jews sold the synagogue site to the Canadian Anglican Mission. This was the first time in over 700 years that someone other than Jews owned the site.

1919   A conference to rehabilitate the Kaifeng Jewish community was held in Kaifeng, organized by Bishop White.

1920   Chen Yuan, a Chinese historian, published "A Study of the Israelite Religion in Kaifeng," which was revised in 1923.

1924   Arthur Sopher, a member of the Shanghai Society, went to Kaifeng and met a Jew from the Zhoa clan.

1926   *Chinese Jews* by Edward Ezra and Arthur Sopher published in Shanghai.

1932   David A. Brown, a prominent American Jew and philanthropist, visited Kaifeng and interviewed local Jews. He published his findings in a series of articles in the *American Hebrew and Jewish Tribune* (January 27–March 10, 1933).

1938   The Japanese occupied Kaifeng. Many residents escaped with the retreating Chinese army. A few reports about the Kaifeng Jews were written in 1940 by Sogabe Shizuo and Mikami Teicho.

1938   Harrison Forman, an American journalist and photographer, visited Kaifeng and took some photos of Jews there.

1939   "The Jews in China: A Bibliography," published by Rudolf Loewenthal. A revised and expanded version was published in 1940. After further research he issued "The Early Jews in China: A Supplementary Bibliography" in 1946, which became the first comprehensive bibliography for the study of Chinese Jewry.

1946   Jimmy Burke and Archibald Steele, two journalists, were in Kaifeng on July 10.

1957   Timoteus Pokora, a Czech sinologist, visited Kaifeng and reported that there were about 100 families with 200 dependents who classified themselves as Jews. He was accompanied by Rene Goldman, an American Jew.

1967   *The Haggadah of the Chinese Jews*, edited by B. D. Drenger (Orphan Hospital Ward of Israel).

1971   *Jews in Old China* and *Studies of the Chinese Jews: Selections from Journals East and West*, both compiled by Hyman Kublin (Paragon Books).

1972   *The Survival of the Chinese Jews* by Donald Daniel Leslie (E. J. Brill) gives a comprehensive scholarly study of the Kaifeng Jewish community.

1975   *The Torah Scrolls of the Chinese Jews* by Michael Pollak (Bridwell Library, Southern Methodist University).

1980   *Juifs de Chine* by Joseph Dehergne and Donald D. Leslie, published by Institutum Historicum S.I. A selection of important letters by Jesuits who visited and interviewed Kaifeng Jews in the seventeenth and eighteenth centuries.

1980   Aline Mosby, a Beijing-based UPI journalist, visited
       Kaifeng and met with several members of the Ai and
       Shi clans for the first time since Pokora's visit. Later on,
       visits of this type occurred frequently.

1980   *Mandarins, Jews, and Missionaries* by Michael Pollak
       (Jewish Publication Society of America).

1983   *Jews in Ancient China* by Pan Guangdan (Peking
       University Press). It was actually written in 1953, but
       remained unpublished until now.

1984   *Jews in Old China: Studies by Chinese Scholars*, translat-
       ed, compiled, and edited by Sidney Shapiro
       (Hippocrene Books).

1992   *Spring and Autumn of the Chinese Jews* by Wang Yisha
       (Ocean Press).

1993   *The Jews of Dynastic China: A Critical Bibliography* by
       Michael Pollak (Hebrew Union College and Sino-
       Judaic Institute).

1995   *Legends of the Chinese Jews of Kaifeng* by Xu Xin with
       Beverly Friend (KTAV Publishing House).

About the Author

Many Jews have studied China, but few Chinese have studied Judaism. Westerners have researched and written about the history of the ancient Jewish settlement in the Chinese city of Kaifeng, but until now, no Chinese scholar with knowledge of both East and West has sifted through, examined, and explained the phenomenon.

While the history of the Jews of Kaifeng is a remarkable story, the history of Xu Xin, Professor of the History of Jewish Culture at Nanjing University, and how he came to be China's leading scholar of Judaica—and the author of this seminal work—is no less so.

When my late husband, Jim Friend, arrived at Nanjing University in the People's Republic of China to teach English in 1985, the first colleague he met as he disembarked from the airplane was a Chinese professor who was teaching a course on American Jewish authors.

Xu had translated works by I. B. Singer, Joseph Heller, Norman Mailer, John Cheever, and Clifford Odets into Chinese. He had written articles on "Saul Bellow and His Novels," "Characters in Singer's Short Stories," "Jewish Humor," and "The Image of the Schlemiel in Jewish Literature" (likening him to the wise fool in Chinese literature).

A former member of the Red Guard in the Cultural Revolution of the late 1960s and 1970s, Xu learned everything he could about Jews and Judaism through American Jewish literature when he began to take an interest in the subject after Saul Bellow won the Nobel Prize.

But he had never met a Jew!

Jim was the first Jew he had ever encountered, and meeting him, Xu later said, was a turning point in his life.

The friendship between the two led to Xu's coming to the United States and teaching at Jim's school, Chicago State University, for two years. During the first of these years, he lived in our Lincolnwood home.

The very first week Xu was living with us, we attended the Bat Mitzvah of a cousin in Milwaukee. Of course, he went along. Later, he wrote of this experience, "It was the first time in my life that I had ever attended any religious service. What I found there was very touching and moving: man's relationship to his fellow man was so beautiful that I began to feel that the Jewish synagogue was nothing but a home which is graced by many customs and ceremonies, illumined by the sacred lights of festivals and cheered by songs of joy and faith."

When the High Holidays were celebrated, Xu attended services with us. On Rosh Hashanah we took him to our synagogue, the Jewish Reconstructionist Congregation (JRC) in Evanston. On Yom Kippur we all traveled to a tiny synagogue in Alpena, Michigan, near the military base where our daughter, Tracy, was then living.

On Simchas Torah we were back at JRC. We wanted him to see and experience the magnificent sight of the Torah unfurled—held, cherished, shared by the congregation. And he marched with us as we celebrated Torah.

And so the year progressed: Purim, Passover.

Of the Seder, Xu later wrote, "The special decoration of the table, the symbols of the feast, the Haggadah readings, meant more than ceremony because it integrated tradition with contemporary values that applied that tradition to modern society."

And all through that year, Xu read books on Jewish history and religious practices. He lectured at an Oneg Shabbat in our temple on the many similarities between the Jewish and Chinese civilizations.

He stated that both are old civilizations that have suffered yet never lost a belief in their own high cultural value; both share strong family traditions and close family relationships; both value education.

When Xu left the United States, he did not hurry back to China. He had always planned to visit England and France on the way home, and now, because of his Judaic studies, he decided to try to add Israel, especially Jerusalem, to his itinerary, because he feared that once he returned to China he might never again have the opportunity.

El Al sponsored his flight, and the Harry S. Truman Research Institute for the Advancement of Peace at Hebrew University covered his expenses in return for a series of lectures at the school on "Jews and Judaism through Chinese Eyes."

He told the *Jerusalem Post* that Israel, to the Chinese, is "an alien and mysterious country, even more so than the countries of the Western Hemisphere," and that what little the Chinese do know is negative. "We learned that Israel was the running dog of the Western imperialist powers," he said.

Despite his extensive reading of American Jewish authors, he acknowledged that, like most Chinese, he knew little factually about Jews or Judaism, as there was practically no literature on the subject in China. In fact, until he came to Chicago, he had thought that Hebrew was a dead rather than a spoken language. Until he visited Israel, he had never heard of a kibbutz.

But Xu's desire to learn more about Judaism did not end with his trip to Israel. Upon his return to Nanjing, he established a China Judaic Studies Association. The subscription list of the newsletter of the organization, which I edit and publish, now includes six hundred individuals and more than twenty college libraries (including the Harvard Yenching Library), the New York Public Library, and a library in Moscow.

The goal of the Association is to further the cause of Judaic studies in China by publishing articles and books on Judaism in Chinese, offering related university courses, as well as seminars and public lectures that promote a better understanding of Jewish culture and the Jewish people, subsidizing publications and awarding Chinese scholars who have made outstanding contributions to the field, building a library for research and study, and organizing domestic and international conferences on Judaic studies.

In addition to the time spent preparing and teaching courses on Jewish culture, Xu has translated In the Heart of the Seas by S. Y. Agnon, and a critical article on him for the journal Contemporary Foreign Literature. This was the first time since 1949 that a Chinese journal published an article on a modern Hebrew writer.

Coincidentally, the Chinese translation of Agnon came out at the same time as the opening of the Liaison Office of the Israel Academy of Science and Humanities in Beijing, illustrating the growing Chinese interest in and involvement with Jews and Israel prior to the official recognition of the state.

Responding to this interest, Xu completed an anthology (with critical introductions and appendices) of modern Hebrew short stories by twenty Israeli writers, including Agnon, Amos Oz, Haim Hazaz, Moshe Shamir, Uri Orlev, Yehuda Amichai, Ruth Almog, G. Shofman, Y. Shteinberg, and B. Tammuz.

But most dazzling is Xu's work on the translation of an abridged version of the Encyclopaedia Judaica, for which he promised the publisher $10,000 to subsidize the work. Xu donated $1,000 of his own money (a veritable fortune in China) and raised funds for the rest. An article in the Jerusalem Post praised Xu as the single most active and productive Chinese scholar on Judaism and noted how daunting the task of fundraising is in a country where the 1989 per capita income of urban dwellers was $275 a year. Funds for the encyclopedia were raised by grants from organizations and individual donations. After being sold out, the work is now in a second edition.

Xu, who studied Hebrew at Ulpan Akiva for three months, had the opportunity to present the first copy of the encyclopedia to the president of Israel.

No subsidy was requested for Xu's next book: Anti-Semitism: How and Why. China is noted for its religious tolerance, and much interest has been expressed in an explanation of how such prejudice could have arisen historically and still exist today.

Xu has been widely recognized and honored for his work. In the summer of 1992, Harvard University invited him to participate in an academic conference on "The Jewish Diaspora in China: Comparative and Historical Perspectives."

Xu has also acted as a guide for American groups touring Jewish sites in China. In 1991, he traveled with Erica and Rabbi Neil Brief and sixteen members of the Niles Township Jewish Congregation on a visit to the ancient city of Kaifeng to learn about the Jews who had lived there since biblical times and to meet some of their descendants. I led another such trip in the summer of 1993.

Xu's first book in English, *Legends of the Chinese Jews of Kaifeng* (KTAV), was published in 1996 while he was in the United States studying the Talmud at Hebrew Union College in Cincinnati and Yiddish at YIVO in New York. He completed his year and a half of studies as a visiting scholar at Harvard, and upon returning to China he led an international conference on Judaica at Nanjing University.

In the summer of 1997, he ran an extraordinary three-week seminar for selected Chinese scholars who were teachers of Western history and civilization so that they could learn about Judaica with the goal of incorporating such knowledge into their courses.

Currently, he has returned to Harvard to complete the manuscript of this book and to begin work on the creation of a complete Judaic curriculum for Nanjing University.

It has been one of the rare privileges of my life to work with such a man—the most productive scholar I have ever known. His work is a mitzvah, building a "Great Wall" of knowledge against the inroads of anti-Semitism.

In explaining one culture to another, he has enriched both.

Beverly Friend, Ph.D.

Index